SECRETS OF GREAT LEADERS

50 ways to make a difference

Carol O'Connor, PhD

First published in Great Britain in 2015 by John Murray Learning. An Hachette UK company.

First published in US in 2015 by Quercus.

British Library Cataloguing in Publication Data: a catalogue record for this title is available from the British Library.

Library of Congress Catalog Card Number: on file.

Paperback ISBN 978 1 473 60954 9

eBook ISBN 978 1 444 79513 4

1

The publisher has used its best endeavours to ensure that any website addresses referred to in this book are correct and active at the time of going to press. However, the publisher and the author have no responsibility for the websites and can make no guarantee that a site will remain live or that the content will remain relevant, decent or appropriate.

The publisher has made every effort to mark as such all words which it believes to be trademarks. The publisher should also like to make it clear that the presence of a word in the book, whether marked or unmarked, in no way affects its legal status as a trademark.

Every reasonable effort has been made by the publisher to trace the copyright holders of material in this book. Any errors or omissions should be notified in writing to the publisher, who will endeavour to rectify the situation for any reprints and future editions.

Typeset by Cenveo® Publisher Services.

Printed and bound in Great Britain by CPI Group (UK) Ltd, Croydon CR0 4YY.

John Murray Learning policy is to use papers that are natural, renewable and recyclable products and made from wood grown in sustainable forests. The logging and manufacturing processes are expected to conform to the environmental regulations of the country of origin.

John Murray Learning
Carmelite House
50 Victoria Embankment
London
EC4Y 0DZ
www.hodder.co.uk

Also available in ebook

CONTENTS

INTRODUCTION

There are almost 520 million Google search hits for the word
'leader', including news stories, features, research, advice,
courses, activities, jokes and books. This doesn't include the
variations of 'lead', 'leading' and 'leadership', so this very big
number could actually be even bigger. This is unsurprising
because people are curious about leaders. The average person
wants to know if anyone can be a leader or is leadership for a
select few? They also want answers to these questions: What
creates leadership success? How should leaders behave? Would I
be accepted as a leader?

People are drawn to the topic because instant communication
makes it so easy to follow famous leaders' activities and watch
them in the news. What these leaders do, say and think is
everywhere – whether on the Internet or on television – and their
behaviour makes many people wonder whether they could do a
whole lot better themselves. Consciously or unconsciously, people
measure and compare modern leaders against one another as well
as against leaders from the past.

Indirectly, this produces a modern popular idea of the ideal
leader. This is fed by the craze for celebrity, where famous
figures from reality television go on to assume leadership
roles elsewhere, and their success makes the idea even more
fascinating. This is a positive trend, because people identify with
their idols and wonder how they can become leaders as well. This
is a good question and one that everyone should ask.

This is because leadership is open to anyone willing to step up
and take responsibility on the day and deliver what is needed. But
anyone who has ever been a leader knows that it's more hard work
than glamour – more like being the last one standing on a sinking
ship than posing under Klieg lights on a red carpet. Leadership is a
rewarding job but the hardest undertaking there is.

Even when events go in a leader's favour, with every decision a
winner and every plan a success, it's only a matter of time until
there's an inevitable downturn. Then it becomes the leader's
task to make sense of the chaos without ever having the money,

people or information to do the job properly. When things go sour, the leader is the only one who has to keep going – always with the belief that there will be a happy ending, or at least presenting a show of this belief.

Others can moan about their misfortune and say 'Why me?' but a leader can't even entertain that thought. That's a part of the job, but when things come right again, there's also a feeling of quiet satisfaction that is like nothing else.

Leadership offers a chance to take responsibility, to stretch and become bigger and better. It forces a person to 'think big and broad' in order to ensure that their choices serve a bigger and broader situation. The leader's task is to develop and maintain the security of those being led. It's not about what the leader can get from the job or the glamour of being the centre of attention. It's about the relationship that develops between the leader and the people being led. Successful leadership will always be measured by the strength of that relationship.

Leaders and followers create a two-way street, with mutual gain for both when the relationship goes well. Together, they create a virtuous circle. The leader's part is to organize the necessary resources in order to support everyone working together. In turn, those being led are productive and get the work done. This supports the leader's original efforts.

The process is repeated as mutual support continues. The circle breaks only if one side or the other forgets that they work together and should be mutually supportive, and that they depend on each other for mutual success. Business leaders who recognize that they work *for* and *with* employees create a positive work environment. Employees who respond to this feel empowered and in turn empower their leaders.

This is called employee engagement and it works like cogs getting into gear. As boss and workers click, there's an understanding of business goals at every level of the organization. People feel their everyday actions are connected to achieving those goals. Employees have a positive attitude towards their work and show this by making suggestions, sharing new ideas, and behaving in a supportive way towards one another. There is a sense of commitment among the workforce and a desire to do a good job. This may sound idealistic, but numerous studies show that smart business leaders are committed to developing an engaged workforce. Decisions are taken at board level to work within guidance from government-backed programmes such as Investors in People to ensure that they get workforce relationships right.

In 2003 Gallup produced a study that included 1.4 million employees across 192 organizations in 49 industries and 34 countries. Gallup found that organizations with a critical mass of engaged employees significantly outperformed their competition, with 22 per cent greater profitability and 21 per cent greater productivity between the top and bottom sections of the organizations that were measured.

This means that an empowering leadership style makes a difference to both profit and productivity. In short, when leaders engage their employees' commitment, the business makes more money at less cost. There are many other studies going back to the twentieth century, all saying the same thing and providing a model for leaders to follow. This emphasizes the leadership skills that show employees respect and also encourage them to grow and develop.

This book of 50 secrets offers tips for becoming this kind of leader – one who listens, speaks well, makes smart decisions, is clever at solving problems, has authority, gets and gives respect, wants personal growth, actively works and co-operates with others, and much more. Its purpose is to advise leaders who want to inspire other people to grow while they maintain their own enthusiasm, happiness and *joie de vivre*.

None of this is easy: the training necessary to become a good leader is ongoing and takes a lifetime. Becoming a *great* leader is even harder, but it is well worth the effort because leadership makes a huge difference to the success of any enterprise. There can be sufficient money, a smart strategy and effective marketing for a great product or service produced by good employees, but without effective leadership it can all fall to pieces.

The three main themes

The 50 secrets suggested in this book support three main themes: practical, visionary and connecting, with takeaways intended to sharpen thinking, enrich life, and develop a network of wholesome and mutually supportive contacts. The secrets are chosen with the aim of helping you organize situations and people, supporting your personal growth and the development of others, and building healthy relationships based on effective communication and trust.

- **Practical**

> *'Common sense is the knack of seeing things as they are, and doing things as they ought to be done.'*
> Harriet Beecher Stowe

This theme is labelled 'practical', but it could also be called 'common sense'. It includes secrets that support taking action and helping leaders to improve the way they function at work. Topics include decision-making, debating skill, using social media, managing uncertainty, disrupting the status quo, dealing with failure, planning, managing time, and others. The idea is to enable leaders to prepare for potential threats and be ready to take advantage of opportunities when they arise.

Improved performance as a leader, however, is still no guarantee of success. Some of the world's great business leaders, politicians and inventors failed many more times than once. For whatever reason, they didn't act on time or didn't recognize impending threats until it was too late. There's a saying: 'Fool me once, shame on you. Fool me twice, shame on me.' Leaders who survive a failure are the ones who have learned from their mistakes. They return with new ideas and the commitment to avoid making the same mistake a second time.

This resilience is inspiring and also a good example of what anyone can do. Failure creates the best leaders, resilient and tough, and also able to accept that other people can make mistakes as well. They know how it feels to lose. They're back, but with greater self-awareness and direct knowledge of what it takes to repair and revive their hopes. A practical approach to leadership sees failure and success as two sides of the same coin. Smart leaders know that whatever happens in the toss, it can be changed with another try.

- **Visionary**

> *'Inspirational leaders need to have a winning mentality in order to inspire respect. It is hard to trust in the leadership of someone who is half-hearted about their purpose, or only sporadic in focus or enthusiasm.'*
> **Sebastian Coe**

When people think of leadership, they often associate it with qualities of vision and inspiration. People admire visionary leaders who show the way to new thinking. This theme also includes topics for personal development and motivation because vision depends on seeing the world as it could be. Old ways of thinking can get in the way and so it's a good idea to decide what still works and what is now outgrown.

This theme includes topics of thinking big, daring to be different, never giving up, and being lucky. These are secrets that support a leader's grasp of a whole situation – rather than its parts – to support their taking action. They show leaders when to choose caution, when to take risks and when to act with a blend of both.

- **Connecting**

> *'In real life, the most practical advice for leaders is not to treat pawns like pawns, nor princes like princes, but all persons like persons.'*
> **James MacGregor Burns**

The ability to make contacts and to work within networks indicates a leader's talent for connecting with others. These are now core skills because leaders in today's streamlined organizations must work through other people. Long and thin chains of command no longer exist. They are too expensive to run, and so leaders need to know how to manage flatter structures with more people for each leader to supervise.

Communication skills, alliance building, creating trust, encouraging people to grow and knowing when to give a second chance are all examples of the secrets included within the 'connecting' theme. Increasingly, the leader's role is to maintain and develop existing connections and ensure that more are made continuously and in support of excellent communication. It has always been important for leaders to have regular contact with a great variety of people, but the speed of information exchange now makes this a core function.

During the night before battle, General Robert E. Lee visited his troops' campsites to meet and encourage as many soldiers as he could before dawn. Napoleon knew the names of all his officers, where they were born, all the battles they had fought and the names of members of their families. Making connections is a core leadership function that is as old as the act of leading.

What happens next?

Before you begin reading, think about what you want to gain from this book. If you're already a leader, ask yourself whether there's a performance area that you want to improve. Or maybe the list of 50 topics will help you identify a new development area. Either way, let your personal interest guide what secrets to read first or which advice may help you more. You may also use the topics that interest you most as starting points for further reading and study. A wealth of information is freely available on the Internet.

If you are new to leadership, ask yourself which secret would help you get started. Then think of a project or situation that will give you a chance to practise what you learn as you read about that topic. Starting small is a good thing. Leading a local charity run or fundraiser is a good beginning. Learn from this and set your sights to gaining a bigger role. Make friends at every stage and stay in touch with them. This is your leadership network and it will bring you big benefits over time.

1 BASE DECISIONS ON KNOWLEDGE AND DATA

'In any moment of decision, the best thing you can do is the right thing, the next best thing is the wrong thing, and the worst thing you can do is nothing.'
Theodore Roosevelt

'Never make a decision when you are upset, sad, jealous or in love.'
Mario Teguh

'No sensible decision can be made any longer without taking into account not only the world as it is, but the world as it will be.'
Isaac Asimov

'The most difficult thing is the decision to act, the rest is merely tenacity. The fears are paper tigers. You can do anything you decide to do. You can act to change and control your life; and the procedure, the process is its own reward.'
Amelia Earhart

'I think it's very important that you make your own decision about what you are. Therefore you're responsible for your actions, so you don't blame other people.'
HRH Prince William, Duke of Cambridge

This secret makes a good starting point because decision-making is an essential for great leaders. Stories about people in powerful positions dominate the media, with leaders' reputations often transformed overnight based on how well they make an important choice. They take the heat and, whether they deserve it or not, they take the blame when things go wrong. Amazingly, people still want the job.

Every leader is driven by personal ideals, a desire for power, fame, or other motives. They want to make a difference, influence others or leave their mark. And given the rewards leaders often receive, their followers are entitled to expect results and an effective performance. A leader's decision-making is the way this can be measured.

Although people don't expect their leaders to have a crystal ball, they do want them to make an effort to get the facts, be smart and use wisdom. Key questions asked about leaders include:

- Do they analyse current events?
- Do they consult with experts?
- Do they anticipate problems and plan how to solve them?

If their decisions are long-lasting and support the majority, these leaders remain popular. Later, if they're proved wrong or their decisions gave little benefit or failed, many leaders retain respect because they acted for the best using all the information available at the time. Particularly if they share with their public that 'These are the lessons learned. We can do better next time', leaders will be forgiven.

By contrast, leaders who delay an important decision or refuse to act on good information and data are never forgiven. Self-interest – or even the suspicion of this – shows a red flag to the victims of poor decision-makers. Some leaders change jobs every two years to avoid the inevitable blow-up from their rushed or poor decision-making. By moving on, they avoid dealing with the consequences of giving big discounts, offering special deals or hiring the wrong people.

Some leaders avoid making decisions entirely. They are like the tortoise hiding in its shell, hoping decision-making challenges will go away. They never do. Others are like sloths, those slow-moving and sleepy creatures, and they delay taking action for so long that the opportunity for making a good decision passes.

In contrast, strong, able and effective leaders take action based on knowledge and data in support of both major and minor decisions. They see this as a responsibility and an important part of their leadership.

Learning the secret of effective decision-making is one of the most important jobs a leader has.

FOCUS ON WHAT'S IMPORTANT

Important first steps for any decision-maker are to understand why a decision is necessary; why the decision has to be made at this time; and what problem it must solve. For example, if you're asked to lead a renovation project, before deciding what to do, you need to know what purpose the renovation is supposed to serve. Is it to:

- upgrade the electronics and communications systems?
- enlarge the workspace for additional staff and new projects?
- modernize the workspace to attract and retain good employees?
- meet new health and safety requirements?

Each of these projects will have a different set of priorities and these dictate what you need to do next. Before doing anything, however, you need to write a purpose statement: 'The purpose of this decision is to...' Then you look at your budget to see whether there is enough money to meet the decision's needs. If not, you need to revisit the decision's purpose and scale down or change your priorities to meet your budget.

This may mean contacting your boss for more information about how to meet the decision's needs. If you are the lead decision-maker, you may need to ask your financial adviser how to raise more money. If this isn't possible, this is when you scale down your purpose. For example, an electronics upgrade can be done in planned stages. When you are clear about the decision's purpose, you are better able to identify the right priorities and deliver what is needed.

GATHER AND STUDY NECESSARY INFORMATION

SWOT is a classic decision-making technique and an acronym standing for strengths, weakness, opportunities and threats. SWOT analyses and organizes information about existing conditions. It also guides your thinking about what could happen in the future. For example, if you have to make a decision about renovating the workplace, and you produce a purpose statement about upgrading the current electronics system, a SWOT analysis will help you identify solutions that support that purpose.

Strengths are what still works in the existing system. Make a list of all the system's good features. Can you build on any of these? If previously purchased parts were good quality, can you buy from the same supplier?

Weaknesses are what is out of date, broken or never really worked well. List these and also ask what went stale or wrong quickly in the old system. Contact people who used the old system and ask them about its weaknesses.

Opportunities are how a new system can create business and increase contact with existing customers. How can you future-proof a new system to give it longer life?

Threats are the potential danger resulting from the new system. How you can protect the business from them? You can use the PESTELI technique described below to explore threats further.

MAKE YOUR DECISION

PESTELI is an acronym standing for seven external factors that can have a big impact on your decisions: *politics, economics, social trends and forces, technology, environment, laws and government,* and *industry change.* By studying each factor's potential influence on your business, you can future-proof decisions.

1. **Political:** Think about the influence your local and national politicians have on your business. If there were changes, what would happen? For example, has your local councillor or your MP been of help? Is there any benefit in looking for their help in future?
2. **Economic:** What would happen to your business if the national economy took either an upturn or a downturn? Is there anything you can do to be ready for this?
3. **Social:** What influence, if any, do social attitudes have on your business? What if people stop wanting what you offer? Do you have alternative ideas?
4. **Technology:** If you are making a major upgrade, how can you ensure adaptability?
5. **Environmental:** This refers to storms, floods and natural disasters of any kind.
6. **Legal:** Are there any new tax laws in the works, such as a change in VAT or new health and safety laws? Will you need price flexibility, at least for the short term, or will you have to make workplace adjustments?
7. **Industrial:** Are there any shifts and changes in your industry that can affect your business? Do you follow industry trends so that you can prepare for change?

Putting it all together

Regular use of decision-making techniques provides a steady source of information in support of both major and minor decisions. Regular practice of these techniques also makes it easier to assess your current circumstances quickly, and gather necessary facts and figures for rapid-fire decision-making.

Decision-making techniques will help you avoid repeating mistakes by challenging your ideas. Experience can count against you if you've become stuck in a fixed routine or have an inflexible attitude. The best decision-makers look for weaknesses in their own plans. They never say, 'We've always done things this way. Why should we change now?'

Routine saves time, but if you count on using the same solution without collecting new facts, you put decisions at risk. Effective decisions need preparation and any method or technique that helps to gather information in a systematic way will support you when you find yourself pressured to decide.

2 FOLLOW YOUR INSTINCT

'People who lean on logic and philosophy and rational
exposition end by starving the best part of the mind.'
William Butler Yeats

'We think, each of us, that we're much more rational than
we are. And we think that we make our decisions
because we have good reasons to make them. Even
when it's the other way around. We believe in the reasons,
because we've already made the decision.'
Daniel Kahneman

'It has been said that man is a rational animal. All my life I
have been searching for evidence which could support this.'
Bertrand Russell

'Nothing defines humans better than their willingness to do
irrational things in the pursuit of phenomenally unlikely
payoffs. This is the principle behind lotteries,
dating, and religion.'
Scott Adams

'Superstition is foolish, childish, primitive and irrational – but
how much does it cost you to knock on wood?'
Judith Viorst

This secret may seem like a contradiction of Secret 1, *Base
decision on knowledge and data*, but it isn't. At times, leaders
lack necessary information but they still need to make important
decisions. This is when their job becomes more art than science
and instinct has to take over. It's when they think rapidly as they
unconsciously process a range of variables in order to calculate
what to do. They are flying at night without radar and somehow
have to make good, and even great, decisions.

This is the golfer whose long experience takes into account the wind's direction and force, along with air pressure, length of shot and a hundred other minute factors before deciding which club to choose and how to strike the ball. The final decision is based on instinct – but that instinct draws on information and data embedded in the golfer's mind. It takes many years of practice to learn to produce an instinctive reaction.

This is also the policeman who, with his partner, drives through a parking lot late at night on a routine patrol. The lot is deserted but for one car and its sleeping driver. Later, both officers described feeling a 'buzz' when their instinct kicked in as, without discussion, they drove slowly out of the lot. 'There was something about the way the car was parked,' said one. 'It was the back window rolled down those two inches,' said the other. Whatever it was that roused their instinct, they immediately called for backup and were able to capture a serial killer without incident.

Leaders of emergency services describe similar experiences when they scope a crisis situation. Their eyes are like cameras recording every detail but avoiding a fix on any one feature. They focus only when their experience tells them where immediate action is needed. They all say that plans don't work when things are blowing up. Instinct does.

> ### Furthermore
>
> Professor Gerd Gigerenzer, a psychologist says, 'Gut feelings ... take advantage of certain capacities of the brain that have come down to us through time, experience and evolution. Gut instincts often rely on simple cues in the environment. In most situations, when people use their instincts, they are heeding these cues and ignoring other unnecessary information.'

UNDERSTAND YOUR GUT REACTION

A gut reaction has nothing to do with your physical gut and everything to do with what scientists call 'rapid cognition'. This is the way the brain blends knowledge, experience and skill to interpret what's happening to you. It's very fast and entirely unconscious. Unlike random guessing, rapid cognition finds clues in the environment to tell you how to react.

You can increase your ability to use your instinct so that it becomes another tool in your problem-solving toolkit. The first step is to watch for physical signals when meeting a new person, reviewing plans or thinking about an important decision. The signal will last less than a second and is the way your body tells you that your brain just registered an instinctive response.

Such signals include:

- sweaty palms
- rapid eye blinking
- a catch in your breath, a small gasp or cough
- a feeling that your surroundings have faded in importance as you notice one item.

Notice and record every signal-type experience you have, even if you aren't sure that you really felt anything. Note any hesitation you may feel as well. Include in your notes the date and a sentence describing what you were doing at the time. When you have several pages of recorded signals, begin studying your notes to identify patterns. The more you do this, the better you'll become at listening to your instinct.

KNOW YOUR LEFT BRAIN FROM YOUR RIGHT

If you're entirely committed to rational thought, you are unlikely to use instinct. If you do, you may even keep it a secret. Or you may ignore it when it happens. However, as already described, research says that your instinct is actually smarter than your rational mind. It hears a subtle tone in a colleague's voice that warns you the colleague is about to quit. It sees an expression on your daughter's face that signals that she's unhappy at school.

It may help leaders who are solely committed to rational reactions to know that the brain is divided into two sections called hemispheres, with each side having a different function.

The left side controls logic and rational thought, and organizes information into a hierarchy. When this side of your brain is in charge, you like step-by-step problem-solving methods, order and structure and planning for the future in some detail.

The right side controls creativity, has the ability to interpret spatial relations, and looks for patterns in data and the environment. It's this pattern-finding function that supports an instinctive response. Scientists monitoring brain activity report that the right side of the brain lights up when a person has an 'Aha!' experience. When the right side of the brain is in charge of thinking, you have easy access to instinct and will be likely to depend on it when making decisions. However, the two sides are well connected and, when information passes freely between the two, instinct and rationality work together.

TAKE A BREAK AND CHANGE YOUR MIND

When you get stuck working on a problem, it's always sensible to take a break rather than endure frustration as your thoughts go round and round. You need to clear your mind of all the ideas you've already considered and forget all the data you've previously collected. It's your left brain that insists you carry on working even when it's obvious you're getting nowhere.

The best use of break time when problem solving is to activate your right brain. This should involve music or physical activity like walking, running or sport of any kind. This is because you depend on your right brain to judge distance and measure rhythm. The right brain also manages hand–eye co-ordination. By doing something your right brain is good at, you turn off your left brain more effectively.

Juggling is an excellent problem-solving activity. It requires eye-to-hand coordination and so much concentration that you are taken entirely away from the problem you're facing. Using a skipping rope is a good choice because it forces your brain to focus on rhythm and timing. It's also easier to learn than juggling. These activities are useful – and not only for break time – because they energize your right brain and increase communication between the right- and left-brain hemispheres. This will stimulate your creativity in the long term and also improve your ability to recognize an instinctive reaction.

Putting it all together

No one wants to be a 'one-trick pony', able to make good decisions or solve difficult problems only when conditions are right. Leaders need flexibility and their instinct gives them this. It allows them to make decisions that draw on all their skills and experience. On occasion, this is necessary because concrete information is unavailable and so without instinct nothing can be done.

Instinct tells you whether something is safe or dangerous and is far more reliable than a logical, left-brain evaluation of people, places or things. It's interesting that some of the same people who insist they are entirely rational also use rapid cognition to solve problems without realizing it. If caught using instinct, they will explain patiently that it was logic after all. But there's no argument against that here. Their right brain studied the data to find a pattern, found it and then fed it to the left brain for a logical decision.

3 MASTER PUBLIC SPEAKING

'There are always three speeches for every one you actually gave. The one you practised, the one you gave, and the one you wish you gave.'
Dale Carnegie

'If you have an important point to make, don't try to be subtle or clever. Use a pile driver. Hit the point once. Then come back and hit it again. Then hit it a third time – a tremendous whack..'
Winston Churchill

'You can't just give a speech and expect people to fall down and agree with you.'
Hillary Clinton

'The most precious things in speech are the pauses.'
Ralph Richardson

'It usually takes me more than three weeks to prepare a good impromptu speech.'
. Mark Twain

Public speaking is one way for leaders to present a message with authority. This secret, as well as Secret 11, *Speak clearly and well*, explains how to improve your presentation skills so that speaking before a large audience becomes both effective and rewarding. If you prefer not to speak before large groups, there are alternatives. Ideas are offered in Secret 8, *Make social media work for you*, and Secret 27, *Write in a simple style using plain language*.

Mumbling, speaking too softly, using distracting gestures or an irritating tone of voice are all traits that can be changed, but this is often a challenge. These mannerisms may appear only when the speech begins and disappear – along with the sweaty palms – when it ends. This is particularly annoying when huge effort goes into preparing a speech with the hope that it will go well. The solution is to learn from past experience and improve each problem area one at a time.

A weak or unpleasant voice can be strengthened with breathing exercises or singing lessons. This can also increase confidence and a sense of calm when you are facing an audience, because breath control can often manage nervousness as well. Another way to address nervousness is to make short presentations regularly to small groups, and then gradually lengthen the time of the talks while increasing the audience size. Annoying habits can change with effort and the decision to do it. There is absolutely nothing to keep a leader from giving a good, if not excellent, speech. As with any skill, public speaking takes practice and a commitment to learn. Finding opportunities to practise may mean something as small as volunteering to introduce a visitor to the team. Every opportunity to speak in front of a group offers valuable experience.

Furthermore

Toastmasters is an international organization committed to encouraging public speaking. It can be credited with encouraging beginner speakers around the world. Business leaders of some of the poorest developing nations say that Toastmasters gave them their start because public speaking enabled them to influence an audience and gave them confidence to compete globally. There are local chapters in 126 countries and becoming a member is a low-cost way to grow as a leader.

KNOW YOUR AUDIENCE AND PITCH YOUR MESSAGE

Rhetoric is an ancient Greek word meaning 'the art of the orator', and it is the art and science of public speaking. Until the mid-twentieth century, less than 70 years ago, it was a required study topic for a university degree. Whatever your profession, you would be expected to know how to speak effectively in public. Journalist Sam Leith recently reinterpreted the topic for modern readers in his book *You Talkin' to Me?*

Leith explains that the purpose of every speech is to communicate a message, and he suggests that, before deciding what to say, the speaker should consider the needs of the situation and the point of view of the audience. These guide the speaker to decide how to make the message as appealing as possible. Leith draws on the origins of rhetoric and describes three ways a speaker can influence an audience:

1. Depend on expertise: give facts and rely on being the expert and an authority.
2. Present a worthy cause or belief that the audience should want to support.
3. Use logic to make a case, step by step, to prove the best solution.

Next, the speaker matches one of the three ways to suit the situation and audience. For example, an audience of lawyers will be more open to a logic-based speech; scientists are better convinced by use of expertise; and voters may be more open to an appeal to their political or social beliefs.

BELIEVE IN YOUR IDEAS

Belief in your own ideas is essential for public-speaking success. You also need to understand your audience and emphasize the benefits your ideas offer them as well as the problems your suggestions can solve. This requires translating your own personal beliefs into a message your audience finds useful and helpful.

Start by prioritizing your key points. Then organize these points in a logical sequence. Your goal is to carry your audience with you as you present your ideas. You should practise until you can look at your audience and speak in a natural way.

Here is a sequence of steps to follow.

1. Identify your message essentials.
2. Consider your audience's potential reaction.
3. Choose one key point to emphasize.
4. Anticipate objections and plan how to encourage agreement.
5. Use plain language and short sentences.
6. Repeat the key idea at least three times in very different ways.
7. Move to the next key idea, and then the next.

This sounds easy, and actually it is if you forget about yourself and focus only on getting your message across. Your conviction, along with strong content that supports your ideas, can be compelling. Public speaking is like storytelling. Each of the key points you want to get across needs a beginning, a middle and an end, with a transition to move the listener's attention to the next key point.

MAKE PEOPLE LAUGH AND FEEL GOOD ABOUT THEMSELVES

Humour brings people together and removes bad feeling. After sharing a hearty laugh, it's very difficult for anyone to stamp away in anger. Although the best source of humour arises from circumstances, story-like jokes also work well in speeches. Even generic humour from the Internet can receive new life if introduced in the right way. For example, as you begin to speak, you say, 'I was on my way here when I heard this piece of news.'

The news can be a funny story from a website, the radio or a news channel that you can link to the audience's current circumstances – adapting it here and there to make it seem funnier. Alternatively, you can create an excuse for adding a joke. One very successful fundraiser does this by telling the audience he has just won a prize for the best joke, and then wonders aloud which one it could have been. He follows this with a series of jokes, told rapid-fire. His speeches always raise more money for charity than expected.

However, ridiculing a minority, a disability or gender difference, or depending on body parts or functions for laughs, is never appropriate – in either life or work. In business, it can and will mark your card as unsuitable for promotion. Eventually, someone in the room will be both offended and have enough influence to hinder your career. Anyone who has ever complained that a ridiculed colleague 'cannot take a joke' needs greater self-awareness.

Putting it all together

Social media and the trend to keep all eyes glued to a screen can make the idea of public speaking seem old-fashioned. Speaking to a live audience could also look inefficient when so many people can be so easily reached electronically. But if the intention is to make an impact and influence opinion, there's no substitute for gathering an audience together in a single place. There is an atmosphere in a gathering, as people arrive and they see who else is present.

People are social beings and the way to reach them is in a social setting. A great speech can inspire and lift a gloomy and doubt-filled audience so that they leave the room in a positive frame of mind. This is an opportunity that every leader should explore. It goes to the heart of why you want to be a leader and shouldn't be missed.

You can be a source of inspiration. Public speaking takes practice but really anyone can learn. It's a skill and is entirely technique-driven. Learn the techniques, speak to an audience as often as people will let you, and gradually you can become the one everyone looks forward to hearing speak.

4 SURROUND YOURSELF WITH SMART PEOPLE

'Associate yourself with people of good quality, for it is better
to be alone than in bad company.'
Booker T. Washington

'I will not let anyone walk through my mind with
their dirty feet.'
Mahatma Gandhi

'Surround yourself with only people who are
going to lift you higher.'
Oprah Winfrey

'When I was a kid, there was no collaboration; it's you with
a camera bossing your friends around. But as an adult,
filmmaking is all about appreciating the talents of the people
you surround yourself with and knowing you could never have
made any of these films by yourself.'
Steven Spielberg

'You can't build any kind of organization if you're not going to
surround yourself with people who have experience and skill
base beyond your own.'
Howard Schultz

Smart people are naturally curious and they want to know why situations develop in the way they do. They're usually not content until they've solved nagging problems, and will miss meals, work late and refuse to give up until they do. They tend to have good relationships at work because they believe that bickering, rudeness and aggression are all a waste of time and energy.

Here are five additional reasons to work with smart people:

1. **The Monday challenge.** You can count on your smart colleagues to think of new ideas for everyone over the weekend. They ask, 'Do you have a minute?' and then present their new idea. Although this can be annoying, their energy is often infectious and, if channelled wisely, is a real benefit to the team.
2. **The performance edge.** Smart people can make everyone else look good. They understand team strategy and take action before being asked. This is useful when they address details you forgot and solve problems without your having to ask.
3. **The raised bar.** A single smart person forces everyone else to raise their standards. Again, this may be annoying if these ideas disrupt long-established routines with ideas that suggest higher standards. But when they point out inefficiencies, you feel forced to improve. This is a good thing.
4. **The extra advantage.** Smart people discover advantages and benefits that enable your team to beat the competition. It's amazing how they look at the same blank wall as everyone else, then effortlessly see a door and open it. They prompt the question, 'Why didn't I think of that?'
5. **The bump-up.** Smart people also make other people look smarter because their creative ideas, insights and behaviour have a positive impact. Seeing the world through their eyes is to gain a bigger perspective.

ENCOURAGE OTHERS TO BE SMART

Start by looking at the strengths and weaknesses of your existing team members. When given a chance to develop, many people become smarter with encouragement and the right training. This works better if there is a specific job they can train to do, or a complex problem that needs to be solved right away. If they have no experience at doing this new work, then you can organze the job into smaller steps that they can take forward.

Working together with your colleagues, to help them discover their own strengths, not only brings value to the team but is also highly motivating to them as individuals. Just the assumption that they have potential can be positive and inspiring. However, you need to use tact when asking about colleagues' future ambitions during a performance review or during a one-to-one conversation. If anyone would prefer not to discuss future plans, you need to accept this.

But if they are willing to talk, you can help. For those with ambitions that seem too low, you can suggest raising their horizon. If too high, you can help them set shorter-term goals. This would support them in moving forward with less risk of their becoming discouraged. The benefit to you is discovering any hidden gems among your team. It would not be the first time that a potentially smart person went unnoticed due to their lack of confidence.

ATTRACT SMART PEOPLE TO YOUR TEAM

A big draw to any team is how it is led. Smart people will endure all kinds of hardship if they believe they are learning, are respected and have an inspiring leader. However, they are also the first to leave when they believe that the hardship is the result of poor leadership. Their smartness tells them that things will only get worse. So you can begin to attract great people by being a great leader.

Another step is to balance your team with a mix of backgrounds, ages and personality types. This ensures variety when brainstorming for creative solutions. Avoid hiring clones of yourself that agree with you. These are not necessarily yes men or women but people who see the world in a similar way to you. Such people are great for social situations, but not for work.

A way to ensure that you recruit people with different perspectives from yourself is to use a framework like the one developed by Meredith Belbin. He puts the personalities necessary for a balanced team into three main categories according to whether they are 'thinking', 'action', or 'people' oriented. Then he further divides each group into three sub-groups so that there are nine types in total. You can learn more about this at www.belbin.com.

The Belbin framework helps you create the right mix by identifying what categories are already represented in your team. You can then actively look for people to balance the team to achieve its goals. You can also encourage people to extend their abilities. If they are action oriented, you can give them work that requires skills from the thinking category. However, this can't be forced and training is likely to be required to ensure that they have a chance of success.

A round peg doesn't fit into a square hole.

KEEP THE SMART PEOPLE YOU ALREADY HAVE

The previous strategy suggests that good leadership draws smart people. It also helps you keep the people you already have, even when your work area offers minimal opportunity for growth. Like migrating birds, smart people readily take off for somewhere better if they find their stopover is unpleasant. But they linger if they like where they've landed. Create the right environment and you may keep the smartest for longer than is usual.

Offering a challenge is a good way to retain your talent. Is there a problem that needs attention but you haven't time to tackle it? Ask for volunteers from your team to study it and come up with three alternative solutions. Let them know that you think it's difficult and that you value their help.

This last idea is essential because smart people like to believe they can do the impossible. Make sure they know in advance that you may not have the budget to action their ideas right away but that, if one of the solutions is good enough, you'll want to try it in future.

Putting it all together

'Smart' as a label can be used to inspire people to try harder and aspire to being smart. In fact, everyone is potentially smarter and better at something. They – and you – need encouragement to take on a challenge just for the sake of stretching existing skills and developing new qualities.

As a leader, you can inspire smart behaviour in everyone so that they:

- solve problems
- organize work – both routine and specialized
- communicate effectively, both inside and outside the team
- learn from one another
- control the use of resources.

These activities can always be done better. Everyone can work smarter, regardless of previous achievement level or professional training. As a leader, you can encourage people to try harder, dig deeper into their talent-and-skill box and pull out a greater performance.

5 KEEP PROMISES AND HONOUR AGREEMENTS

'It is easy to make promises – it is hard work to keep them.'
Boris Johnson

'Hypocrisy can afford to be magnificent in its promises, for never intending to go beyond promise, it costs nothing.'
Edmund Burke

'An ounce of performance is worth pounds of promises.'
Mae West

'Promises are like crying babies in a theatre, they should be carried out at once.'
Norman Vincent Peale

'Your life works to the degree you keep your agreements.'
Werner Erhard

Promises are commitments, and failure to keep them creates a good reason not to trust the promiser. It doesn't matter if 100 promises were kept; people will remember only that one failure, colouring everything else the promiser does. It's so important to keep a promise that it's better to say as soon as possible if it seems likely that it can't be kept.

This is true in principle, and especially true when making a promise to someone who could be needed in the future. This may seem cynical, but it's just common sense. There are only 24 hours in the day and often there are more things to do than hours available, so it's a good idea to decide which promises are most important. If someone has to be let down with a broken promise, it's better to consider in advance just who this may be.

Start by thinking about which relationships are most important. Is it family, friends or colleagues? While numerous studies show that people are happiest when they make family their priority, this is difficult when deciding whether to leave colleagues to finish a major project in order to attend a child's piano recital or football game. At times putting family first just doesn't seem to be an option.

As a general rule, it helps to create a hierarchy of importance. Try to keep promises to those at the top of this hierarchy most often when tough choices must be made about letting people down. Managing expectations can help. When making a promise, think about what could go wrong and explain this to the person receiving the promise. It's the responsible and right thing to do and the other person deserves this information.

Furthermore

Kept promises are the glue that holds people together. Until the 1980s in the City of London – the financial centre of the UK – the expression 'My word is my bond' meant that deals could be settled with a handshake. The business world was smaller then, and a reputation for honesty could be gained among financial colleagues more easily than today. Now reliability is just as important, but individuals must prove they are reliable only one promise at a time.

RECOGNIZE WHAT PROMISES MEAN

A promise is an agreement to act in a certain way, or an assurance that a thing will or will not be done. It invites another person to expect an outcome resulting from your behaviour. Breaking even a small promise can lead to serious consequences for the other person and relationships have failed simply because one person kept another waiting in the rain for just ten minutes.

Mind you, the promiser who complains that the ten-minute wait was reasonable in the circumstances may choose not to mention that their lateness is a habit, that it was actually 30 minutes and was in a raging storm, and that the person waiting for them was attacked and robbed. A difference of opinion about the importance of a promise goes to the heart of why it's so important to keep them.

There's also often a difference in motivation between the person asking for a promise and the promiser. The desire or need for a promise to be kept is far higher for the person asking than for the person promising. Before promising anything, make sure that you know what it will mean to the other person if you cannot deliver. This is more than managing expectations; it's ensuring that you understand the degree of importance.

If it's highly important, than you need to ask yourself realistically how likely is it that you will fail. If it's highly likely and it's highly important, then it's better to say you cannot promise. Be clear and explain the facts. You can suggest alternatives to the promise; you can be tactful, but saying no is the more supportive action when the risk of failure to deliver is high.

ENSURE COMPLETE UNDERSTANDING

Emotions run high with promises, and so it's smart to clarify exactly what is being promised. A misunderstanding creates the same disappointment as a broken promise, and can also lead to the same loss of faith and relationship breakdown. Kept promises show that a person is valued. Broken ones show disrespect. This can be unreasonable when confusion or vague wording leads to a failed delivery.

You may promise to attend a meeting on behalf of your colleague, but receive the wrong address and so go to the wrong place. This is not your fault. In fact, it's the other person's fault. But if they lose a major contract because you didn't show up, unfairly they will blame you. Likewise, a supplier gets caught in traffic and fails to deliver a crucial piece of equipment, which then results in your losing a client. Would you decide not to use that supplier again?

A classic technique that helps to ensure understanding is to ask the other person to repeat what you just said. This will reveal any confusion, missing information, or emphasis on the wrong features so that corrections can be made. When a promise is very important to the person asking, a five-minute pause to ensure understanding is both smart and justified. Both parties should do this.

DON'T MAKE THREATS

A threat is a hostile promise. Instead of making a commitment to do what the other person asks, the person making the threat is committed to doing something the other person doesn't want at all. It's a negative commitment. Very often, its purpose is to frighten and remind others of their potential weakness. 'If you..., then I will...' is a sentence intended to chill the other person into obedience.

Like all promises, it's linked to emotions and this in itself is dangerous because emotional reactions are so unpredictable. Truly anything can result when you threaten. The risk of escalation is high. Some people refuse to be threatened as a matter of principle. They see it is as so serious a loss of face that they would never accept a threat. Others decide to return the threat and, if they are angry enough, will try to do lasting harm to the person making the original threat.

Buried deep in the brain is an almond-shaped mass of cells called the amygdala. This small brain part manages fear reactions and the initial response to a threat. It's considered a primal feature of the brain and is the source of rage and bursts of temper that can overcome a person. Although we may usually control our primal reactions by choosing to behave civilly, even a minor threat may cause sufficient fear to override reason. This issue alone should be enough to avoid making threats. Because of the amygdala, you can never guess how someone will react when threatened.

But threats can also be necessary. If you are invaded or feel under threat yourself, you have to take action to assert yourself. Keep in mind that language can either inflame or soothe: you can give the same message in different ways, to cause either fury or relaxation. Explain – calmly – what your reaction will be if the person does what they threaten. Make sure that this is something you can and will do immediately.

Putting it all together

Your reputation for reliability results from keeping your promises. You're seen as someone to count on, someone to trust. It's a great feeling to know that your behaviour has made a positive difference. Like a pebble thrown into the pond, your kept promise affects all the people who benefited from each ripple outward from the original promise. It also bonds you to the person to whom you kept your promise, reassuring him or her that they are valued. When other people feel valued, they in turn value you.

Some people will take advantage, of course. They have no intention of keeping even the smallest promise. Lizard-eyed, they say, 'Sure, I'll pick up the papers on my way to the office. It's on my way.' Then the idea goes out of their heads as soon as they have said it. What they gain from making promises they won't keep is anyone's guess. If this sounds like one of your colleagues, it's best mentally to put them in quarantine. Listen and smile, for sure, but never take their word for anything.

6 SEE THE PERSON, NOT THE STEREOTYPE

'People are incapable of stereotyping you; you stereotype yourself because you're the one who accepts roles that put you in this rut or in this stereotype.'
Eva Mendes

'We shouldn't judge people through the prism of our own stereotypes.'
Queen Rania of Jordan

'Ethnic stereotypes are boring and stressful and sometimes criminal. It's just not a good way to think. It's non-thinking. It's stupid and destructive.'
Tommy Lee Jones

'Once you label me you negate me.'
Søren Kierkegaard

'Yeah, I had gay friends. The first thing I realized was that everybody's different, and it becomes obvious that all of the gay stereotypes are ridiculous.'
Bruce Springsteen

A stereotype is a fixed idea about a group of people that gives them a single, shared identity. There are no individuals in a stereotype because everyone within it has the same strengths and weaknesses. Stereotypes can be positive, such as 'tall people are leaders', or negative, such as 'unemployed people are lazy'. They are also never true. A stereotype cannot be accurate because, after all, it's an attempt to generalize about an entire body of people – without exception.

There only has to be one tall person in the whole world who refuses a leadership role for the stereotype to be inaccurate. As nonsensical as they are, stereotypes are widely used. They save time because they offer a guide to assessing other people: 'That man is wearing a suit like my own. I'll talk to him because we'll have things in common.' This kind of unconscious thought doesn't make sense, but it makes people feel comfortable and often drives social exchanges.

Stereotypes can also be cruel, particularly when an entire group is consistently passed over for recruitment, promotion or any other advantage. Only if members of the stereotype are socially and financially independent of their victimizers can they ignore the limits being placed on them. Even in this case, being stereotyped is an uncomfortable experience and can seriously undermine a person's confidence.

Many stereotypes are learned from family, with children's views being shaped without their making a conscious choice. This is why people are often unaware that they are using stereotypes, and honestly don't realize the harm they are doing. Only if they make a racist or other objectionable remark, and are then criticized for it, do they realize that there may be a different way of thinking.

It's important for leaders to realize that stereotypes work like filters that exclude, expand or minimize information at the very point their brain receives it. Stereotypes disable the ability to see and hear accurately, and trick perception so that experience is distorted. Even positive stereotypes are harmful because looking at anyone through rose-tinted glasses creates false expectations and potential disappointment.

UNDERSTAND HOW PERCEPTION WORKS

Perception is the way people organize information so that they are able to understand what's happening to them. It's how people learn and it often occurs like this:

1. They have an experience they've never had before.
2. They feel confused and look for more information to interpret this experience.
3. They piece the information together and produce a story or idea to explain it.
4. They store the interpretation for the next time they have a similar experience.

For example, the first time a child sees a big metal box on wheels, carrying a lot of people, they don't know it's a bus. After learning what it is, they don't need to relearn that fact every time they see it. Instead, whenever one rolls along the road, they can shout, 'There's a bus!'

Everyone has perception. It goes along with having five senses, but individuals have unique ways of sifting through and filtering information. This begins at birth and continues as they copy family members' reactions and behaviour. Gradually, they learn from the people around them what has value and also how to interact with others. They form attitudes towards foods, thunderstorms, religions, ethnicities or lifestyle choices, as well as hundreds of other things to be in favour of or against.

This is all normal and healthy. It's only a problem when people close their minds and develop rigid beliefs. They ignore evidence and distort information to reinforce their original and unchanging point of view.

JUDGE LESS AND UNDERSTAND MORE

Judging removes you from the conversation. It sets you above other people, cutting you off from an exchange of views. You may continue talking aloud but inside you feel removed, as if you are watching without getting involved. You've made up your mind and there is no further need to think about the issue. This is why the legal system places judges on a raised platform. Once seated in court, the judge's job is to observe the evidence and avoid an emotional reaction.

But sitting in judgement in everyday life is a trap that everyone falls into at some time. It happens like this: you see something, lack the necessary information to understand it fully, fail to realize this lack, and interpret the event as either positive or negative. You then react by making a judgement about it without checking the accuracy of your interpretation.

The magic bullet that stops judgement in its tracks is always more and better information. Understanding the meaning of what you see allows you to connect with it and have a genuine emotional reaction to it – good or bad. This all occurs consciously and, as soon as you understand, the judging stops. The two reactions of judging and understanding are incompatible; by far the better and smarter choice is to understand.

Judging increases the danger of stereotyping. Understanding stops it and supports an open mind.

IDENTIFY YOUR OWN STEREOTYPES

Even well-meaning people use stereotypes. These stereotypes may be harmless references such as 'That newspaper says too much about...' with a mention of sport, fashion, negative stories, politics from the opposing side, or other topics. They could be innocent generalizations about food preferences, such as 'The Irish love potatoes', or 'The Scots love their oats.' There can't be any harm in this unless it breeds a mental habit of generalizing about a person, place or thing. Then it can gradually lead to a closed mind and rigid thinking.

Stereotypes may also result from a painful experience with a type of person or even a location. The usual result is ignoring that person, place or thing. This may also be the right course of action if you've learned that cutting the person off is the safest choice.

However, stereotyping can develop unconsciously. Here's a checklist to review your own attitudes:

1. Make a list of all the stereotyping labels you can think of, both negative and positive and including those you would never use or say aloud. ☐
2. Ask yourself how you feel when you hear this label or see it printed in the media. ☐
3. Try to remember when you first heard this label. This is difficult but offers some interesting information about your current reaction to it. ☐
4. Is there a way you can create a positive experience with the person, place or thing associated with this label? ☐

Putting it all together

Some people suggest that stereotypes are harmless, that they save time, make people feel safe, and help identify interest groups. There may be a bit of truth in this, but stereotypes generally do much more harm than good. Until you have experienced being the odd one out or the unwelcome square peg in the round hole, you cannot know how painful it is to be limited by a stereotype.

The leader's job is to bring everyone forward together. It's easier to do this when people are encouraged to express their individual qualities. This enriches any team effort and develops the creative atmosphere necessary for problem solving. Long gone are the days when leaders commanded an army of clones. No one will accept this now.

The best teams are made up of strong individuals. Stereotypes get in the way of this. Everyone needs to see the unique skills and qualities of everyone else and get the best out of their work experience. This approach also ensures diversity and shows that a company avoids discrimination. When none of the '-isms' can gain a toehold, it's going to be a happier and healthier workplace.

7 SET HIGH STANDARDS

'Don't compromise yourself. You're all you've got.'
Janis Joplin

'If you are going to achieve excellence in big things, you develop the habit in little matters. Excellence is not an exception, it is a prevailing attitude.'
Colin Powell

'There is no passion to be found playing small – in settling for a life that is less than the one you are capable of living.'
Nelson Mandela

'Excellence is never an accident. It is always the result of high intention, sincere effort and intelligent execution.'
Aristotle

'It's hard to be a diamond in a rhinestone world.'
Dolly Parton

In sport, 'personal best' refers to an individual athlete's best score, time or distance. The goal is to beat this *best* score and then replace it with a tougher number as soon as this happens. A personal best allows athletes to watch their own development and drives them to a better performance. It's a healthy way to compete, and is much better than focusing on a competitors' strengths and weaknesses. What others do becomes less important than going after a personal best as the highest standard to follow.

A standard is a rule or principle used to measure whether a specification is met. It's also an agreed way of doing things and a guide that a level of quality has been achieved. BSI, the British institute that maintains industry and management standards, says, 'Standards are knowledge. They are powerful tools that can help drive innovation and increase productivity.' This sounds very like a personal best and the reason why athletes want, seek, use and need to set personal performance standards.

Although standards are useful for determining whether a goal has been reached, they aren't the goal itself. Goals differ from person to person and serve an individual's purpose. For example, two swimmers both enter a race willing and able to conform to the race's standards and do their best in the water. However, one of the swimmers is recovering from injury and just wants to stay competitive while regaining strength. The other wants to win and also beat a personal best.

The swimming contest serves them both. The racing standards offer a context for the competition. Within that, swimmers can channel their energy to achieve their goals. Any set of standards works in the same way. High standards at work measure quality for production, services or human performance. However, there are leaders who want to achieve a personal best within the context of their workplace standards. They're happy only if they are pursuing their own best result.

KNOW WHERE STANDARDS COME FROM

It's a good idea to know the source of the standards you follow. Those imposed by an external authority – such as work, school, social or family – should harmonize with your own talents and abilities and stretch you to develop further. In some cases, these externally imposed standards are too low; in others, they can be impossibly high or even misguided, time wasting and harmful.

Take a moment to think of the standards you follow. Ask whether you chose them because they:

- stretch your abilities
- match your beliefs and values
- give you an opportunity to try something new
- test your skills against objective criteria.

If you answered yes to all four questions, your chosen standard is likely to support further growth. If you answered no to any of them, take a step back and consider the standard's source and also what drives you to want to meet it. Some standards are the result of perfectionism, where you have a drive to do things perfectly all the time, with zero tolerance for failure.

The need to be perfect gets in the way of genuine improvement. This requires accepting, studying and learning from mistakes. Athletes conscientiously study each performance to identify every fault in order to do better next time. Perfectionism gets in the way of analysing a performance because failure is too distressing.

CHART YOUR ACHIEVEMENTS

This activity requires you to think about the stages of your life. In proportion to your age, divide your lifetime into three segments. For example, if you're 30 years old, the segments are 1–10, 11–20 and 21–30. Please identify your achievements within each segment.

1. Divide a piece of paper into three segments, labelled *early*, *middle* and *progressing*.
2. In the *early* segment, think of ten milestones you remember as important, such as starting school, playing games or meeting people outside the home.
3. Ask yourself what made you feel proud, embarrassed or determined. Circle those items.
4. Were you aware of having standards? Were they imposed from outside or did you choose them for yourself?
5. In the *middle* segment, identify another ten milestones.
6. Again ask yourself what made you feel proud, embarrassed or determined. Circle those items.
7. What was the source of those standards? Were they created by yourself or imposed from outside? Did you believe they were high, low or appropriate? Circle those you believe were suited to the circumstances.
8. In the *progressing* segment, identify another ten milestones.
9. Again, ask what made you feel proud, embarrassed or determined. Circle those items.

10. Did you ever feel driven by standards set by external sources? When, how and where did you set your own standards? How did your performance compare, between your own and external standards?

EVALUATE WHAT YOU WANT IN YOUR LIFE

Look at the items you listed in the three segments from the previous activity. Are there any that you feel particularly proud of achieving? Do they have anything in common with each other? It's also interesting if they are entirely different. Look for patterns of behaviour and repetitions of achievements throughout all three segments. Take notes on your reactions for study later.

Next, reflect on any connections between the milestones you achieved and the source of the standards you followed. What drove you to work to those standards? Some drivers include:

- feeling great afterwards
- winning a prize
- being the centre of attention
- making your family proud
- gaining experience.

All drivers are useful as long as you know what they are.

Blindly going after a goal and training to a high standard can produce a severe let-down if you discover, on winning, that it's not what you want after all. Decide first what you want in life and let that determine the standards you should follow. If your goals are demanding, then you need higher standards than if your goals are easy. There is no right or wrong about this, but successful leaders feel inspired by going after big goals and meeting tough challenges. They like high standards because they require a stretch to achieve them.

Putting it all together

Standards set leaders apart. When they are positive, they receive praise, promotion and new opportunities. Alternatively, when weak, they can result in loss and frustration. There are people who call themselves unlucky because they don't see a connection between the way they behave and the situations they create.

At times, standards become habits and these can be good or bad. It's worth taking time out regularly to think about what you do and the way you do it. Look at the results you create and then decide what benefits you get from the way you perform. Standards can also create a rut, with spinning wheels and little progress. Even high standards can hold you back if they are out of date and need to change to meet new challenges. Although changing habits of mind or action is difficult, it's worth the effort.

Perfectionism creates another problem and is actually an enemy of excellence. This is because a perfectionist works to the extreme: at one extreme avoiding self-evaluation entirely and at the other extreme becoming self-obsessed. Self-acceptance of all your faults and gifts is the better starting point for examining your personal standards. Understanding your strengths and weaknesses and accepting them will help you decide what to change and how to do it.

8 BENEFIT FROM SOCIAL MEDIA

'The number one benefit of information technology is that it empowers people to do what they want to do. It lets people be creative. It lets people be productive. It lets people learn things they didn't think they could learn before, and so in a sense it is all about potential.'

Steve Ballmer

'Smartphones and social media expand our universe. We can connect with others or collect information easier and faster than ever.'

Daniel Goleman

'Everybody gets so much information all day long that they lose their common sense.'

Gertrude Stein

'Back, you know, a few generations ago, people didn't have a way to share information and express their opinions efficiently to a lot of people. But now they do. Right now, with social networks and other tools on the Internet, all of these 500 million people have a way to say what they're thinking and have their voice be heard.'

Mark Zuckerberg

'Electric communication will never be a substitute for the face of someone who with their soul encourages another person to be brave and true.'

Charles Dickens

Wikipedia founder Jimmy Wales wants all knowledge to be available and easily accessible to everyone. He says the purpose of the online encyclopedia he developed is to make 'a world in which every single person on the planet is given free access to the sum of all human knowledge.' This builds on the twentieth-century idea of universal education so that, in addition to an ability to read, every single person also has access to a vast global library.

Social media is one way to access all of this knowledge, with many platforms and networks such as Facebook, Instagram, Twitter and Pinterest acting as communication channels. They make sharing information and ideas very easy and raise people's expectations of what they should and could know. In some cases, however, these channels have also lowered expectations: ten years ago, did anyone want to know what a famous politician eats for breakfast? LOL.

Increased access to information also supports business by offering ways to describe and promote a company's products. At the same time, it allows customers to demand higher standards of service and quality. Instant access to a network makes it easy for a customer to warn hundreds and even thousands of others to avoid one place and visit another. This benefits everyone because companies now have a more realistic idea of how to succeed.

More than 20 years ago, the World Wide Web Consortium, a charitable organization founded by Sir Tim Berners-Lee and leading technologists, debated whether to allow commerce on the Web. Happily, they decided that their new invention was to be used by all for free. It was then that the search began for how it could benefit business. This is all so obvious now: people buy, sell, teach and share both things and ideas all the time, and they accept that being connected to everyone else is normal.

Social media is the natural development of Web-based activity. Instead of just visiting web pages, people interact with them, and millions of conversations take place in real time. This is another game-changer, with a new emphasis on mobile apps and constant connectivity rather than PC search. And it is happening so quickly that it's impossible to predict the future benefits – and risks – for business.

DECIDE WHAT'S PRIVATE

Of course, there will always be stupid people tweeting cruel remarks or sharing private information as if only one or two of their BFFs can see. LOL when they later tweet that they had no idea they would cause offence. There are also many smart people using social media to promote personal or business brands and who create a potential tsunami of support for their trending ideas. All this is great, but it's worth trying to figure out where this all may be heading.

It's inevitable that there will be a pulling back from all the compulsive sharing. Those under 15 years old now declare Facebook to be uncool. Mark Zuckerberg, its founder, has begun to promote reading physical books, and telling his many Twitter followers that it's great to read. Further, all the aforementioned stupid people are learning to stop and think before sending a private tweet to the public at large.

These attitude changes towards social media usage will continue, as individuals decide where their personal boundaries begin and their public life ends. There's now a backlash as well against mobile telephone addiction, once again driven by the young, who have grown up with SMS text. It's a utility to them, not a novelty, and they would rather die than say, 'They would rather die without their phones,' as they've heard their slightly older siblings say.

INCREASE YOUR SOCIAL CAPITAL

Whuffie is a reputation-based currency invented by Cory Doctorow for his science-fiction writing. The future world he describes has limitless abundance and people can have whatever they need. What everyone wants, however, is social status, and Whuffie points determine this. Whuffie can be either gained or lost through social interaction and this is determined by a person's positive or negative actions, their contribution to their community, and what people think of them.

Tara Hunt, an expert on promoting business through social media, takes the Whuffie idea a step further. She says that transactions in the digital world depend on reputation, your Whuffie. For example, if you want to sell through one of the major online retailers, your potential customers first check your customer satisfaction scores before buying. If you've acted fairly in the past, this leads to more sales.

Tara Hunt says this is a way to amass social capital and is a form of Whuffie. Although it won't pay for your groceries, it's available to you when you want to ask strangers to trust you when they make an online transaction. In the same way that a glowing reference from a former employer isn't a new job, it has value because it can help you get one. Hunt suggests that you can grow your Whuffie in three ways:

1. **Be nice** when making online contacts and avoid negativity.
2. **Be networked** by increasing your presence in online communities by answering questions, giving advice or offering support.
3. **Be notable** so that your online activities make a valuable contribution and you are recognized for them.

BECOME A CONNECTOR

A connector is a person who brings people together. They are like the host at a big party, greeting everyone as they arrive, remembering who is already there and helping people meet one another for conversation and sharing. The main criterion for the role is an interest in other people and a willingness to put a little time and attention into making life slightly easier for other people.

At work, this is the person who tells you that a job has just come up which sounds like your ideal position. In social situations, it's the person who introduces people who are likely to get along. It may be the neighbour who says that there's a course you may like at the community centre. Connectors are also good organizers and likely to schedule a car pool to work or shared rides for the school run.

Returning to the idea of Whuffie, a digital world connector has high levels of social capital. Taking an active role in the digital world is the first step to becoming a connector. Join the same networks as the people you admire: learn what they do and how they react to both negative and positive events on the network.

If you model yourself on people who are generous to their communities, in a short time you, too, will have social capital. The result will be new business opportunities.

Putting it all together

Social media is an outstanding invention. It's changed the way people connect and therefore the way they relate. This is very good because it leads to greater transparency. News about poor or dishonest service can be immediately sent out. Emergency services can receive real-time information. People can find one another at low to no cost. Education and training are transformed as students working remotely can ask experts questions and get fast answers.

For business, it's the opportunity to gain feedback and promote products and services. As a connector, you have the chance to increase business as a result of your great reputation. Social media can future-proof your business growth because you will always be among the first to know what is happening. The few but serious negatives include privacy invasion, a celebration of superficiality, and the potential for political and commercial disinformation. Managing these risks is the next big challenge.

9 FOLLOW THE RULES YOU SET FOR OTHERS

'If you obey all the rules you miss all the fun.'
Katharine Hepburn

'Serious sport has nothing to do with fair play. It is bound up with hatred, jealousy, boastfulness, disregard of all rules and sadistic pleasure in witnessing violence. In other words, it is war minus the shooting.'
George Orwell

'We learned about honesty and integrity – that the truth matters... that you don't take shortcuts or play by your own set of rules... and success doesn't count unless you earn it fair and square.'
Michelle Obama

'You don't learn to walk by following rules. You learn by doing, and by falling over.'
Richard Branson

'Chess helps you to concentrate, improve your logic. It teaches you to play by the rules and take responsibility for your actions, how to problem solve in an uncertain environment.'
Garry Kasparov

Social attitude is divided about the importance of following rules. Some people believe they are made to be broken, and others think they exist to be kept. But most people place themselves somewhere between these two extremes. This is unsurprising because rules come in so many different forms and serve such a variety of purposes. Rules may be related to religion, engineering, mathematics, art, fashion, government, sport, school, health, social life or grammar, among many other areas.

Some rules truly are made to be broken. Media headlines show delight when fashion or artistic rules are ignored. Language teachers are less pleased but accepting when creative expression breaks a few rules of grammar. Unjust social rules are legitimately defied in peaceful protest when the protesters believe it benefits their society. In contrast, other rules must be kept. It's a scandal and potential tragedy when engineering rules are broken, resulting in the collapse of a bridge or building. And breaking governmental rules – or laws – may lead to a fine or even a jail term.

Recent research about breaking rules shows added complications. When health workers, who fully agree to hygiene rules, work long hours in an intense environment, they wash their hands less frequently than patient safety requires. This is alarming because these workers want to follow the rules but tiredness and time pressure get in the way. How likely is it that those who don't agree with rules will follow them when they experience similar long hours and high-stress situations?

There can be contradictory rules for big companies whose operations are spread around the world. For example, health and safety rules in Brazil are different from those in the United States, and both countries' rules differ again from those in the European Union. An international corporation with offices in all three regions has a challenge when setting its own guidance for obeying national laws.

In addition, there are motivation issues when leaders set rules solely intended for others to follow but not themselves. These are the rules that are most likely to be broken by even conscientious people – those who never break the law – when they are sure that they won't be caught. Unless a leader has unlimited time and resources to police potential rule breakers, it's better to avoid lopsided rule making. Once made, even minor rules like 'No hot drinks in the newly carpeted meeting room' must be followed by everyone. Otherwise, it's guaranteed that eventually everyone will break them.

IDENTIFY GROUND RULES

Ground rules are a starting point and are usually a list of expectations about behaviour that apply to a specific situation. Examples include:

- No smoking inside the building
- Break times to be no longer than ten minutes twice a day
- Don't interrupt one another during discussions
- Mobile phones to be turned off during meetings
- Show respect to difference (race, gender, age, disability) at all times
- Turn off the lights when ending the day's work.

In general, ground rules are useful because they explain how things are done. When new people join an organization, clearly presented ground rules make it easier for them to fit in and get along with everyone else. Ground rules minimize disruption because they guide everyone to work towards a common goal. They also avoid wasting time and money when they spell out the steps necessary to get a job done.

However, the risk is that a leader or a majority group sets rules that serve themselves. For example, a dishonest subgroup in an organization can make a rule that financial records are confidential and no one can question the figures, or a rule that a minority group is paid less or shown less respect. In general, any rule that harms a specific group needs closer examination.

ENGAGE WITH OTHERS WHEN SETTING RULES

People are more likely to follow rules they help create because any failure to do so produces widespread indignation. Peer pressure takes on the job of policing so that compliance among groups of peers is often very efficient.

The following activity explains how to create ground rules in a group situation.

1. Encourage everyone to list existing ground rules – including unspoken ones such as those about styles of dress, parking spaces and sharing the cost of biscuits.
2. Ask what is missing. If necessary, ask everyone to work in pairs to identify new rules or make explicit rules that some follow and others do not.
3. Discuss the suggested ground rules and do a sticker vote so that each person can put stickers on three of the new rules they believe are best.
4. After the session, type out and make copies of the high-scoring rules and distribute them to everyone involved in the discussion.
5. Wait at least a week – never rush into setting rules unless it's a genuine emergency.
6. Have a second discussion to decide which rules, if any, are most useful.
7. Ask what penalties or forfeits would be best when the new ground rules are broken.
8. Issues to consider: is there a grace period while everyone gets used to the new rules; does an honest mistake count as a broken rule; what should be done if anyone ignores the rules?

BE HONEST WITH YOURSELF

Mary overheard her two sons, both under ten, using swearwords she didn't think they knew. She showed them a jar and said that from now on, whenever they swore, they would have to put ten pence into the jar. If they didn't have the money, they were to write an IOU and pay the jar out of the following week's pocket money. This was a serious threat because they each received only a small amount of money per week, which had to cover even their school expenses.

Later that same day, after the boys were in bed, Mary had an argument with her sister. As they became more heated, the older boy woke up. Standing in the doorway, he said, 'Mum, I've counted you and Aunty swearing 30 times. Are you going to put money in the jar?' Mary was stunned. It had not occurred to her that she would have to stop swearing as well.

Rules made in the heat of the moment do have that effect. You see the need for a rule and say it aloud, not realizing that everyone will assume that the rule applies to you as well. Because you don't see yourself as part of the problem, you'll come down with a bump when you're faced with a rule that no one likes – including you. The answer is to ask yourself, before you set any rules, what it would be like to follow this rule yourself.

Putting it all together

There's a joking one-liner that goes, 'The golden rule of work is that the boss's jokes are always funny.' This is true. The more powerful the leader, the easier it is get people to laugh at his or her jokes. Fake, phoney and other words come to mind, but self-deception can happen to anyone. It starts for some leaders innocently. Because they are paid more, receive better benefits, get positive attention, and are flattered by people who want something from them, they can lose perspective.

Gradually, their status and all the extras become natural, and the need to be, or at least seem to be, fair fades in significance. An important reason to follow rules you set yourself is the positive effect this has on other people's motivation when you do it. For anyone who wants a long and happy career, with the respect of colleagues and friends, keeping perspective is the wisest course. It keeps your feet on the ground and it won't even cross your mind that rules are just for others.

10 ASSUME YOU HAVE ENEMIES

'You have enemies? Good. That means you've stood up for something, some time in your life.'
Winston Churchill

'I can be on guard against my enemies, but God deliver me from my friends!'
Charlotte Brontë

'Love your enemies, for they tell you your faults.'
Benjamin Franklin

'Forgive your enemies, but never forget their names.'
John F. Kennedy

'Without a trace of irony I can say I have been blessed with brilliant enemies. I owe them a great debt, because they redoubled my energies and drove me in new directions.'
E. O. Wilson

The word 'enemy' looks old-fashioned on the page. It implies drama, confrontation and attack. World leaders and politicians have enemies, but not leaders in everyday life who work in teaching, the public sector or business – unless, that is, they set out to create them.

For example, E. O. Wilson, the eminent scientist, seemingly set out to make an enemy of Richard Dawkins, another scientist. In a recent interview, Wilson called Dawkins a 'journalist' who writes about science – a remark that is calculated to be insulting in the scientific world. Dawkins then tweeted a series of indignant replies. Why would Wilson do this to Dawkins? Photos of Wilson show a smiling and pleasant-looking man. Admittedly, Dawkins looks less so, but both appear to be mainstream, even ordinary-looking people.

Economists are another group of people who tend to insult one another in public. There's a long list of rivalries, with boffins challenging one another in very rude terms. No sooner does one pop up to smear another's ideas than the rival responds. This is not as entertaining as watching the fights of actors and media people because economists are harder to understand, but it's always amusing to see enemies square up in public.

They must want or like the notoriety or, in fairness to them, they may be driven by the importance of what they have to say. Winston Churchill said, 'Kites fly higher against wind, not with it.' There are occasions when leaders believe so strongly in an action or idea that they disregard the risk of making enemies. This can happen over causes such as a change to local zoning law, a merger of companies that creates a monopoly, or an investigation into corruption.

The secret is realizing that enemies can easily result when people are annoyed by other people's actions. The more driven a leader is to make a difference or leave a legacy, the more likely it is that someone else won't like it. If they really don't like it – for whatever reason – then they can become an enemy. This may not happen, but as the stakes get higher the likelihood increases. It's also often the case that the dislike won't always be rational.

AVOID MAKING ENEMIES

Specialists who advise on developing new markets through social media often skim over the very real risk of upsetting someone. There are Internet trolls out there, and the result of their dislike can range from a 'not like' vote against a comment you make, to escalated flame-throwing at your every comment, to your acquiring an actual stalker.

Social media is a great marketing channel for promoting your business but you should follow a few basic rules to make sure that you, your business and your reputation are safe.

1. Never 'not like' anything, ever. You may be found. It's not worth it.
2. Avoid any reference to politics, religion, social class, race, age or any of the -isms. Even positive remarks about topics can be misunderstood. Trolls are irrational.
3. If you are attacked – even if unfairly – do not respond. Bullies feed on reaction. If they don't get this, they move on to their next potential victim.

You may think, 'What's left to discuss?' That's easy – it's your business and the product and service you offer. Feature feel-good stories and anecdotes about your team. For example, upload photos to your blog or send them to the local newspaper with a story about members of your company helping to clean up a local nature trail. But avoid any reference to a belief in protecting the environment or conservation. There's a subtle but big difference between the two stories.

This isn't cowardice. You need to choose your battles carefully. There will be times when you do want to make a stand. If you are drawn into committing resources to address attacks from Internet trolls or if you have been misunderstood in the local press, you won't have time to give your attention to fighting for the things you believe are truly important.

FIGHT BACK HARD WHEN NECESSARY

Sir Richard Branson famously fought British Airways in the mid-1980s, when the larger company launched a dirty-tricks campaign against his airline, Virgin Atlantic Airlines. The hostility began in 1984 when Virgin began flying to North America. Prior to this, BA was the only UK airline with these routes. From BA's point of view this meant that every passenger that Virgin gained was one that BA lost.

A few years before, Sir Freddie Laker, founder of no-frills Laker Airways, had also competed against BA but had gone bankrupt in 1982. Laker blamed BA and others for a conspiracy to put his airline out of business, also with dirty tricks. When Virgin began to experience a similar campaign, Sir Freddie warned Branson to fight back hard at the first and at every subsequent sign of attack.

So when BA accused Branson of a publicity stunt when he complained about BA's business practices, Branson sued the company for libel. His case included detailed notes he'd personally taken during every meeting either with BA's personnel or about BA's actions. His team also gathered testimony from customers that BA had poached their Virgin flights, as well as how this was done. The result was a detailed dossier of a dirty-tricks campaign, including the distribution of rumours and misinformation to Virgin customers.

When Sir Freddie was first attacked in the late 1970s, he failed to respond in kind. Later he sued BA, but only after his company had gone bankrupt. Although he won a multi-million out-of-court settlement from BA, it was too late for his business. Branson won while Virgin Atlantic was still viable, and is reported to have distributed the multi-million-pound settlement among Virgin employees.

The lesson from Sir Freddie to Sir Richard – and to you – is simple. The instant you are under attack, you act to protect yourself. Avoid escalating trouble, but stop invasion at all costs. Trouble does not get better or go away. Deal with underhand actions with open and public self-defence. Take notes, be dignified, and do not give up.

BE TRANSPARENT IN ALL YOUR DEALINGS

Every business has legitimate secrets. This could be a special list of suppliers or clients, a formula, patents, or intellectual property of any kind. Transparency refers instead to disclosing information that rightfully belongs in the public domain. It usually means revealing business practices and procedures. Transparency makes it easy for people to see what you are doing and why you do it.

For example, your customers know when they will receive the goods they order, and your suppliers know when you will pay them. Your record keeping is accurate and information available to those who have a legal right to see it. This also creates greater efficiency so that you and your business also benefit. Transparency announces that your business is trustworthy. This is essential in these days of social media when dishonesty is so easily defeated by a digital campaign.

Transparency also protects you. If a business rival ever attacks you, your records speak for themselves. Sir Richard's open business style also inspired loyalty among his airline's customers. They came forward voluntarily to testify against BA, while BA suffered because its own lack of transparency created mistrust.

Putting it all together

Knowing you have enemies puts you in a position of relative safety. This is because complacency is your real enemy. Another is assuming that bad things won't happen to you because you're a good person. There are people who want what you have. There are others who are just greedy, angry or misguided. At any time this kind of person can act against you. It may seem strong to call them enemies, but they are certainly not your friends.

In business, as in life, being aware of the forces taking shape around you helps you learn what to do and how to act. The Chinese general Sun Tzu, in his influential treatise *The Art of War*, said, 'So it is said that if you know your enemies and know yourself, you can win a hundred battles without a single loss. If you only know yourself, but not your opponent, you may win or may lose. If you know neither yourself nor your enemy, you will always endanger yourself.'

11 SPEAK CLEARLY AND WELL

'Speak clearly, if you speak at all; carve every word before you let it fall.'
Oliver Wendell Holmes, Sr.

'Talking and eloquence are not the same: to speak, and to speak well, are two things.'
Ben Jonson

'Better to remain silent and be thought a fool than to speak out and remove all doubt.'
Abraham Lincoln

'The real art of conversation is not only to say the right thing at the right place but to leave unsaid the wrong thing at the tempting moment.'
Dorothy Nevill

'To be able to ask a question clearly is two-thirds of the way to getting it answered.'
John Ruskin

Like Secret 3, *Master public speaking*, the focus here is using the voice effectively. This secret is about the mechanics of speech: use of tongue, teeth, jaw and lips to ensure that every word is formed correctly. Those who are speech impaired will probably have already explored the ideas presented in this secret. For other communication methods, refer to Secret 8, *Make social media work for you* and Secret 27, *Write in a simple style using plain language*.

Clear pronunciation is essential for leaders because they often need to give precise directions and explain complex issues. When each word is clearly spoken, listeners follow along. In contrast, they can miss vital information if they have to guess words and phrases that are poorly pronounced. As more information flows in their direction, keeping up and understanding are much harder than necessary.

Regional accents, educational and cultural influences create a variety of speaking styles. Whatever a person's background, speaking clearly minimizes the risk of misunderstandings. If your colleagues can hear each word as it is spoken, they can ask what unknown words mean. They have a starting point to understand what's been said. Alternatively, if they can only hear a stream of sound, pronounced with an accent different from theirs, they simply get lost.

It is possible for everyone to improve their speaking ability. Some of history's great orators began their careers with speech problems: a stutter, a weak voice or poor stamina. They overcame each of these personal obstacles with commitment and determination, inspired by the wish to influence others, be recognized as an authority and create a legacy of their ideas.

Furthermore

Demosthenes was a fourth-century-BC Greek orator. When growing up, he had a speech problem, was frail and was under the control of dishonest guardians. To cure his speech impediment he spoke poetry with pebbles in his mouth, strengthening his tongue, cheeks and jaw muscles. To improve his vocal strength, he gave speeches while standing along the shoreline until he could hear himself above the sound of the crashing waves. Finally, at 16 years old, he sued his guardians and won control of his fortune with an inspired speech. His story shows that the starting point is less important than the decision to improve.

LISTEN TO YOURSELF

This strategy asks you to listen to yourself speak at length so that you have a current sample of your voice to evaluate. It may feel awkward and even strange, but a first step to creating change is identifying how you sound now. Recording is unnecessary for this first sampling because the task is to listen to yourself as you speak aloud. Later, when you try again, you can record this.

First, choose any topic that interests you. Make sure that it's one you can speak about enthusiastically, energetically and with feeling, for example sports, politics, family members, friends who either consistently support you or let you down. Any subject is fine as long as you have a great deal to say about it once you get started. Next, find a quiet place in a setting where it would be acceptable to be found talking to yourself. Now begin to talk.

You may need to warm up to your subject. You may even find it difficult to start. Persevere. You need to have at least five minutes of listening to your own voice. The idea is to hear yourself so that you notice when you catch your breath, run words together, leave letters off words or mumble. These are all mechanical errors that can be fixed with effort. If you find it is too difficult to think of things to say as you speak, read something aloud instead. This takes the pressure off so that you can concentrate only on your voice.

IDENTIFY MECHANICAL ERRORS

After you listen to yourself long enough to get an idea of the way you speak, answer the following questions about breath control, clarity and flow. Be ruthless: the purpose is to discover where you can improve – making excuses for your mistakes won't help you fix them.

Breath control

- Do you take a deep breath and speak until you run out of air?
- Do you stop every so often to take a big breath and then carry on?

Clarity

- Do you slide over some words, blending them together into one long word?
- Do you leave out parts of words or any of the letters?

Flow

- Do you stop between words where a break is unnatural?
- Do you rush your words and ignore sentence or phrasing breaks?

If you answered yes to any of these six questions, you've found areas for improvement and you can begin to work right away. If you're not sure, or even if you answered no to all, repeat this activity while recording your voice. On replay, answer the questions again to find weak areas. Even if your speaking ability is great, you still have room to improve your speech mechanics. Work on one weak area at a time until you notice an improvement. Then begin to work on the next weak area.

UNDERSTAND HOW SPEECH IS FORMED

It can help to know how speech is formed before trying to solve any problems. Speech is produced when your vocal cords, located at the back of the throat, close inwardly, while the muscles of your larynx, located at the front of the throat, tighten. This stretches the cords, causing them to vibrate when air passes through on its way to your mouth. Once air is in the mouth, tongue, teeth and cheeks shape the vibration into words.

A relaxed throat is important because this allows air to flow easily through your vocal cords and avoids unnecessary tension in your larynx muscles. This tension often results in strangled speech, cut-off and half-expressed words, and sudden breaks mid-sentence.

Mumbling and low volume can also result from a tense larynx. This may also happen when insufficient air is drawn from the lungs to pass through the vocal cords. If this occurs, there is less vibration. The mouth needs vibration to form and then project words. Less air passing through the throat and into the mouth means less projection.

Once vibrating air reaches the mouth, the teeth, cheeks and tongue shape the words. Weak tongue and cheek muscles cause mispronounced words. Jaw muscles also need to work because they control the teeth's opening and closing. To illustrate, say the word 'tango' with your teeth held apart. Your teeth do all the work for pronouncing the letters d and t. As you work on your speech, you'll notice greater strength developing in your cheeks and jaws. This will further improve the clarity of your speech.

Putting it all together

Leaders need to be understood; otherwise their message is lost. This secret is about speech mechanics rather than the content and quality of ideas, and is an often ignored skill. It's difficult to listen to your own voice because this distracts from the process of turning ideas into words. You may have to struggle with this at first, but the result is worth while. You need information about how you speak before you can improve it.

It's a revelation to some people that they mumble. When they learn this, they realize that they've blamed others for not listening when their poor speech mechanics is the source of the problem. When poor speakers are also leaders, their more junior colleagues may choose not to ask them to clarify what they just said or to repeat a word. They feel too intimidated by the boss to do this.

So many unavoidable mistakes are made due to a leader's mumbling, frozen tongue and lips, choked throat, weak breathing and other issues. All these problems can be fixed with practice and exercise.

12 PLAN THE LONG TERM AND WORK THE SHORT TERM

'Chance favours the prepared mind.'
Louis Pasteur

'Never doubt that a small group of thoughtful committed citizens can change the world. Indeed, it is the only thing that ever has.'
Margaret Mead

'Twenty years from now you will be more disappointed by the things that you didn't do than by the ones you did do. So throw off the bowlines. Sail away from the safe harbour. Catch the trade winds in your sails.'
Mark Twain

'Choice, not chance, determines your destiny.'
Aristotle

'It takes as much energy to wish as it does to plan.'
Eleanor Roosevelt

This secret in part refers to the expression 'Think globally and act locally', where leaders need to work with local communities as well as be aware of the global issues that directly or indirectly affect their business. This means shuttling attention from the small to the big, and vice versa, to look for connections and insights. It's a skill that needs to be learned and the best leaders have it.

Following traditional news outlets is essential, as well as subscribing to blogs that explore news stories in depth for their impact on industries and sectors. Blogs vary in quality and so it's worth looking at the background of the blogger. Join professional or business societies to stay in touch with changing trends, tax issues and new competition. This covers 'thinking globally'.

Local issues are equally important when looking for business information. In addition to joining a national organization, leaders need to build relationships with their communities. They should join the local chamber of commerce or other local business groups. This kind of society is a valuable source of information about proposed changes to zoning laws or local development plans.

This sounds like a lot of joining, but having professional relationships with other businesspeople is a widely accepted way to create growth that builds on local knowledge as well as national contacts. There's no easy or instant formula to ensure that the business stays current and moves with the times. Joining with others does help.

Furthermore

This secret builds on Secret 1, *Base decisions on knowledge and data*. That secret explains the importance of identifying a decision's priorities and recognizing the spirit that the decision is intended to serve. This secret is about making plans that turn a decision into reality, so that weekly, monthly and yearly goals all work together. The small leads to the big and the big shapes decisions about the small.

Planning for the long term and working on the short term is an efficient way to run a business, saving time and resources by avoiding wasted and redundant effort. It's like sailing a boat at sea. The captain looks to the horizon and heads the boat to its destination while also adjusting the sails and helm in order to get there. Planners, like sailors, need a horizon view as well as the skills to steer the boat.

IDENTIFY THE GAP

The horizon view is your strategic goal and you need to take three steps before you make plans to achieve it. These steps are:

- recognize where you are now.
- clarify where you want to go.
- analyse the gap between your starting point and your desired destination.

This is 'gap analysis', a technique that helps compare the difference between your current and future performances. Once you identify that gap, you can set long-term goals to close it.

It's usually a good idea to start with financial figures. If you work for a large company and are a leader of a division or department, the figures you start with refer to your budget allocation for annual expenditure. If you are a business owner, you need figures for current revenue, profit or another performance measure of your choice. Write these numbers on a page. This is your starting point.

Now ask yourself what numbers you want to achieve. This is your target figure and represents your ambition for the business. Those in corporate roles can identify a future figure that would allow them to achieve more. If they have had a budget cut, this lower figure has to be their future target.

Finally, look at the gap between actual and hoped-for performance. If the gap is too big, the target should be lowered. If the gap is not ambitious enough, you should raise it. Set long-term goals to achieve the target. Those in corporate roles can use gap analysis to meet changes to your budget. Cuts can mean setting goals that lower expenses.

PLAN LONG-TERM GOALS

'Long' and 'short' are relative terms. In strategic planning language, long term refers to setting goals that should be achieved in three to five years. Short term means goals that support the longer term and are achievable in one year or less.

This strategy focuses on identifying long-term goals and the next strategy explains short-term goals.

Long-term goals are headlines that focus attention on getting where you want to go. A frequently made mistake is creating too many of them. This is like a newspaper that shows lots of short news articles on the front page: the reader doesn't know where to begin. It's better to identify a few main goals that clearly take your strategy forward. Under these main headlines, you can then identify actions that serve these headlines.

There are five categories you can use to produce long-term goals. These are products and services, finance, markets, people and facilities. There should be just one single and critically important goal for each category. For example, if your strategy is to expand your sales to China over the next five years, then each of your five long-term goals needs to be general enough to keep your existing business viable while also expanding sales to new markets.

Here are examples of long-term goals for each category:

- **Products and services**: design products and services for international markets.
- **Finance**: update financial systems.
- **Markets**: identify the needs of potential customers.
- **People**: recruit professionals with appropriate skills and knowledge.
- **Facilities**: renew supply chain and distribution solutions.

PRODUCE SHORT-TERM GOALS

Using these five categories and general language to describe long-term goals offers a framework you can use when deciding on specific actions you need to take. Each long-term goal will require many short-term goals to make things happen. For example, the first long-term goal, *designing products and services for international markets*, requires knowing what new customers may want to buy. This is also a *markets* goal.

You avoid wasted time and resources by recognizing right away that you need more information about your new market before designing anything new to sell. Each long-term goal should be developed in harmony with the others, and it's your short-term goals that make this happen.

Short-term goals are usually called SMART goals and each should meet these criteria:

- **Specific**: define what needs to be done.
- **Measurable**: identify a standard that gauges how much progress is made.
- **Achievable**: assess whether it can be done.
- **Relevant**: decide whether it serves long-term goals.
- **Time-bound**: set a deadline for its achievement.

A SMART goal for developing this example's strategic goal would be to gather data about Chinese consumers (S) showing demand for similar products (M), from sources you know you can access (A) that tell you what you need to know (R) within a specific time (T).

Putting it all together

Leaders need to plan for the future, and the most effective way to do this is to identify a strategic goal, then produce a headline describing each long-term goal. These headlines will broadly direct the business to achieve the strategic goal. Each long-term goal then generates a network of short-term goals that are action oriented and make the long term a reality.

Keeping your long-term goals general gives you flexibility. This avoids committing resources over a long period for actions that may fail to produce results. You keep your options open but keep them inside a framework. For example, expansion internationally allows you to shift attention to a neighbouring nation if data is more readily available about its markets, or if it looks more attractive in comparison to the original new market idea. SMART planning keeps you light on your feet and ready to move quickly.

13 FACE CHALLENGE FEARLESSLY EVEN WHEN AFRAID

'Courage is what it takes to stand up and speak. Courage is also what it takes to sit down and listen.'
Winston Churchill

'Courage is being scared to death... and saddling up anyway.'
John Wayne

'You gain strength, courage and confidence by every experience in which you really stop to look fear in the face.'
Eleanor Roosevelt

'Courage is not the absence of fear – it's inspiring others to move beyond it.'
Nelson Mandela

'Courage is the most important of all the virtues, because without courage you can't practise any other virtue consistently. You can practise any virtue erratically, but nothing consistently without courage.'
Maya Angelou

People who choose to stand firm and face danger when everyone else is running away are hailed as heroes. They are acknowledged as special because for most people fear awakens a survival instinct called 'fight or flight'. Adrenaline pumps fast into the bloodstream and the usual response is to run away from danger in a herd, even though it is uncertain who or what is in pursuit.

Those who do stand firm, when questioned later about their moment of choice, rarely mention courage. Instead, they explain they only hoped to keep standing. Firefighters are a good example of facing terrible odds but overcoming their fear. More than 100 years ago, Chief Edward Croker, the modernizer of the New York City Fire Department, said:

> Firemen are going to get killed. When they join the department they face that fact. When a man becomes a fireman his greatest act of bravery has been accomplished. What he does after that is all in the line of work. Firefighters do not regard themselves as heroes because they do what the business requires.

Everyday situations also cause fear but in less dramatic ways. What frightens one person may mean nothing to another, and reactions are unpredictable. Someone may repeatedly face their fear but suddenly reach a tipping point and experience dread, doubt or uncertainty. Externally all can look well, but internally they may be a bundle of nerves.

No one knows what it costs others to face a challenge. Whether it's facing an angry picket line, encouraging demotivated clerical staff, saving a life, or removing a spider from the kitchen sink, each person's challenge is unique. Real heroes are also men and women who fight terrible illness or support their families by taking three jobs to find a way to pay their bills.

Fear is an emotion and so it doesn't help to try controlling it with reason. It's better to understand its source and decide on each occasion whether there is any real danger. If the danger actually exists, match it with caution and preparedness to meet its challenge. If it is entirely irrational, respect the fear, but take steps to work through it.

DIVIDE A MAJOR CHALLENGE INTO SMALLER SEGMENTS

A challenge is an invitation to compete, a confrontation, or a need for great effort to resolve a mental, emotional or physical problem. A challenge often causes fear because you don't know whether you can actually win through. The challenge may defeat you and failure can be yet another source of fear.

Facing the risk of failure like this can feel overwhelming.
A solution is to divide what you have to do into segments and convince yourself that each step is achievable. This creates a step-by-step approach and gives even the most overwhelming task a sense of routine. Here's an example of what you can do to create steps to face your fears.

First, write on a piece of paper what it is you have to do as if it were a headline in the newspaper. 'Young professional starts new business with very little money' is an example of a big enough challenge. Next, decide what 'starts' means, for example clearing the kitchen table for your paperwork or renting a business office. Then you have to clarify in detail what your business will do or what you plan to offer.

This should take time and will lead to other steps, including deciding on your legal structure, identifying your customers, considering whether you should barter for an exchange of services with other professionals, and so on. The idea is to manage how you react to a major challenge by exploring each part of the project step by step.

FOCUS ON THE END RESULT

You can use mental discipline to change your thoughts when you are doubtful about your abilities. Visualization is a technique that helps avoid negative thinking by picturing the outcomes you want and seeing yourself achieving them. It's also a good way to maintain motivation and keep your momentum going. Athletes often use it to create a belief that they can compete and win.

Visualization involves closing your eyes and sitting in a relaxed position in a quiet place where you won't be interrupted. If you feel comfortable closing your eyes, do this. If you prefer keeping them open, drop your gaze and look at a spot on the floor. Next pay attention to your breathing, counting *one–two–three* and thinking of the numbers as you breathe in and then thinking of the same numbers as you breathe out.

Sitting quietly, closing your eyes, and breathing slowly and deeply are first steps to help you feel calm and relaxed. Next, think of your challenge and ask yourself what is the most positive and best outcome you could have. You may be able to picture this, but some people think of a positive story rather than see images in their mind. The point is to imagine yourself winning your goal and meeting your challenge.

UNDERSTAND YOUR FEARS

Fear starts in the brain as a reaction to a trigger from the environment. If the brain has interpreted this trigger as something stressful, it immediately releases cortisol into the blood in order to increase heart and breathing rates to prepare the muscles for an energetic activity: *fight or flight*. The trigger could just be the sound of wind in the chimney, a cat screeching at night, or even a genuine threat to safety.

Ignoring fears or pretending they don't exist is unwise because the fear reaction is a survival instinct. A fearful person is really someone who has yet to learn how to distinguish between serious and trivial triggers. Instead, their brain reacts equally to all triggers, which results in them feeling anxiety and fear as a normal state.

Exercise, a balanced diet, keeping a pet, enjoying friendships and family life are all frequently cited ways to maintain a healthy lifestyle. They are also ways to protect yourself against experiencing unnecessary fear, triggered by unusual or sudden sounds, strange behaviour in others, or chaotic situations.

Good health and happy relationships lower heart rate, make steady and regular breathing your normal state, and at the very least provide a sense of safety in numbers. These are the best protections against fear.

When fear is understood and accepted as part of life, it is easier to identify ways of managing it when facing a major challenge.

Putting it all together

Challenge is part of a leader's life. You can't avoid it and it's very likely that you want to experience it. It's the same drive that makes you seek a leadership role that causes you to look for and accept new challenges. Fear and nervousness can come along with this. For those who face danger as part of their job, facing fear is also part of their everyday lives.

The secret is to develop a healthy attitude towards fear. Like challenge, it's an unavoidable part of every leader's life. If you accept this, then you can learn better to face it. Never ignore your fear or avoid thinking about it. This risks it taking you over at a critical moment. Always know what causes your fear and what events tend to make it grow.

You may not have any control over these events, but you can prepare for them by relaxing into each situation. Fear feels different when you breathe easily, your muscles are relaxed, and you watch events unfold through clear-sighted vision. Creating a sense of personal calm is a big challenge in itself, but it will enable you to face the challenges of leadership more easily.

14 USE TIME WISELY

'How did it get so late so soon? It's night before it's afternoon. December is here before it's June. My goodness, how the time has flewn. How did it get so late so soon?'
Dr Seuss

'Time is the coin of your life. It is the only coin you have, and only you can determine how it will be spent. Be careful lest you let other people spend it for you.'
Carl Sandburg

'Don't spend time beating on a wall, hoping to transform it into a door.'
Coco Chanel

'The ability to lead a happy life is made, not found.'
Martin Luther King, Jr.

'Your time is limited, so don't waste it living someone else's life. Don't be trapped by dogma – which is living with the results of other people's thinking. Don't let the noise of others' opinions drown out your own inner voice. And most important, have the courage to follow your heart and intuition.'
Steve Jobs

Brad Phillips sprints across the car park to make his first meeting, beginning the day as he means to go on – about 20 minutes late. He's been up since 5 a.m. to work on a report he's scheduled to present in Geneva, he's also made several international calls, and helped his daughter with her homework and his wife prepare school lunches for their three children. He enjoys doing it all, but it all takes precious time.

Taking a side entrance, he heads for the back stairs, hoping to avoid meeting colleagues and getting caught in a conversation.

Everyone has something to say, question or promote. 'No time, no time,' is Brad's constant thought, and it's true; he has no time. His life is packed with family, projects, colleagues, ideas, inventions, papers and reports, so that he feels as if he's running on a treadmill at high speed.

His wife has given up asking him to slow down. All she does now is make sure that he eats well, gets exercise and stays in good health. Brad laughs off her concerns although he knows she's right. He also makes sure that he has breakfast with his children every day. He's often home so late that they are long in bed. Being there at breakfast ensures that he takes an active part in their lives.

Added to this, he's been offered a promotion that would mean his having to live in a different city for part of the week. He likes the idea of the added creativity the job would offer, but knows that it will cut even further into his family time and that his wife will be very unhappy with the idea. Brad can't remember when he's had a carefree weekend with his family, and the new job would take up hours of weekend time.

As he reaches his office, he decides to cancel half his morning appointments and put time into thinking about his priorities. He wants more time with his family, creative time to solve current work problems, social time with his work colleagues, time to play football with his friends and enough time to walk slowly across the car park and through the company's front door.

BASE PRIORITIES ON WHAT YOU WANT IN YOUR LIFE

This is an activity to help you decide priorities based on what you want in your life.

1. Cut an A4-size piece of paper into thirds. Fold each third in half and cut at the fold to get six pieces of paper. Then cut each of the six in half to get 12.
2. Make a list of the things you do regularly or daily. Here are examples: exercise, eat meals, take walks, enjoy nature, play music, have a hobby, travel to work, and do your job.

3. Write one of these activities on each piece of paper – so that you have 12 activities on separate pieces of paper.
4. Cut another A4 piece of paper in half. Write on one half 'My ideal life'.
5. Look at the 12 activities written on the pieces of paper. Decide which six are most important to you. Put these on to the paper labelled 'My ideal life'. There should be no overlaps and so only six activities should fit.
6. As you do this, you may think of other activities more important to you than the six already chosen. Substitute these new activities for those less important to you.
7. Think about what you want most until you know which six are the most important activities in your life.

Organize your life so that you give quality time to your six priorities.

DELEGATE TO CREATE MORE TIME

Deciding what to delegate and to whom is the first step to freeing time.

1. List what you do during each hour of the working day. Include work from several days so that you have more information to consider.
2. Decide whether each hour was spent on administration and routine matters, or on future planning and strategy. Put activities that don't fit into a third category called 'Other' – but try to avoid using this category because things like meetings can be strategy or administration, depending on the meeting's content. Problem solving can also refer to administration or strategy.
3. Write A, S or O against each hour.
4. Total the time you spent on administration and strategy, and ignore any work you labelled 'Other'.

To decide whether you are using your time wisely, use the following guide for balancing administration with strategy at each organizational level.

- Junior level: spend less than 10 per cent of your time on strategy.
- Middle level: spend about 50 per cent of your time each on administration and strategy.
- Senior level: less than 10 per cent of your time should be spent on administration.

Based on this model, decide which parts of your work you should delegate and to whom. Make sure you discuss the delegation idea fully with the person. Then explain why it's important and also why it needs to be done within what timeframe. Get agreement that the work is understood and that the deadline can be achieved. Failure to take time to explain almost guarantees failed delegation.

DECIDE WHAT QUALIFIES AS URGENT

When your business is in crisis, you know that it's not the time to tidy your desk. Instead, you focus quickly on what needs to be done. If you've never experienced this kind of crisis before, then your first step is to identify very quickly what is most urgent and then act on this decision.

Focusing your mind like this is an 'awareness shift', and you learn how to do it only by having to lead during a time of crisis. It means expanding your attention so that you can see the whole situation in a single panoramic shot. This skill is crucial in a crisis because there's the risk that an isolated feature can appear vital when there is a mass of potentially confusing information to manage. A panoramic shot clarifies a situation.

Judgement and common sense are helpers, but mental preparation is even more important. The right mental attitude helps you to believe that everything can be done, in the right order, the right way, and in the right time. Why? Because it must. This attitude keeps you calm. Although your mind is working at speed, outwardly you may seem quiet and steady.

Mental preparation gives you this attitude. Take time out regularly to think about what could go wrong in the different areas of your work and your life generally. Identify likely weak points where a crisis could cause real damage. Consider how you would cope if any of those weak points actually broke. These are your 'urgency points' and, as time allows, you should fix them in advance.

Putting it all together

There's a lot written about work–life balance and how best to spend the 24 hours a day that everyone is given. Each person's 24 hours can be a mindless treadmill, a meaningful walk, or a march forward full of purpose. It can also be a mix of all three. Events can seem out of a person's control when actually they are the result of a series of choices all leading to that moment.

For example, deciding to spend time at the pub instead of studying in the library is a choice that beings predictable results. The same is true when someone chooses to work excessive hours and so has limited family time. Genuine economic need often drives long hours, but this means that it's even more important to choose how to spend time outside work.

Work–life balance means choosing what goes into your life first and then balancing this with a constant evaluation of your priorities. Although it may be difficult at first to decide what those priorities are, it's the most important thing anyone can do. Deciding to do more or less of something can be critical to a happy life.

15 HAVE A SENSE OF HUMOUR

*'Good planning is important. I've also regarded a sense
of humour as one of the most important things on a big
expedition. When you're in a difficult or dangerous situation,
or when you're depressed about the chances of success,
someone who can make you laugh eases the tension.'*
Sir Edmund Hillary

*'A person without a sense of humour is like a wagon without
springs. It's jolted by every pebble on the road.'*
Henry Ward Beecher

'When humour goes, there goes civilization.'
Erma Bombeck

*'Keeping an active mind has been vital to my survival, as has
been maintaining a sense of humour.'*
Stephen Hawking

'I don't trust anyone who doesn't laugh.'
Maya Angelou

A sense of humour is another of the essentials for leadership, but
what exactly is it? What about people who don't get jokes, never
laugh, and look blank in situations that are very funny to others?
Can they be leaders too? And if they can, are they at a disadvantage
compared with leaders who do find things funny? Finally, is a sense
of humour the same as being able to make other people laugh? It's
all a big puzzle with more questions than answers.

Certainly Zen masters, Anglican bishops, philosophers, scientists,
police and many others have all said that leaders must be able to
laugh at themselves and see the funny side when things go badly.
This ability, when analysed, looks as if those leaders take a step
back and see themselves and their situation in a bigger context.

This is in contrast to fixing on details, never looking around, and wanting to remain a very serious centre of attention.

E. B. White, the children's author and journalist, said, 'Humour can be dissected as a frog can, but the thing dies in the process and the innards are discouraging to any but the pure scientific mind.' When someone says, 'I don't get it,' after hearing a joke or funny story, it takes willpower to resist describing what is funny. It's just possible that the funniness will survive the explanation, but this will be an exception. Humour needs to be spontaneous.

It also depends on point of view. Here's an example of what happens when two people have different ideas of humour. A man is overheard complaining about British people laughing too much. 'Why do English laugh when nothing is funny? I say a thing and they laugh. Why do they do this?' His companion then explains the Blitz Spirit and that laugher so often brings the nation together during difficult times. Unfortunately, the man then answers indignantly, 'I am not a bleetz!' causing his companion to laugh and the man to stamp away. This story may also make some readers laugh, but – critically for this secret – not others. Why would that be? Scientists and psychologists have long discussed what makes people laugh and they haven't got any answers, or rather any answers worth reporting here.

TELL JOKES

Seriously, jokes are wonderful ways to connect with friends, strangers and an audience large or small. They are also great to read when you are on your own, just to make yourself laugh. However, if you're new to telling jokes, you do risk feeling silly the first 10 to 20 times you try, but laughter so often follows that it's worth the effort. The uplift and energy you feel following a burst of laughter can become a little bit addictive.

Laughter is entirely wholesome and healing, and a joke's sole purpose is to produce it. This makes jokesters pretty marvellous people. All you have to do is learn a few in order to join the joke-telling club. The best jokes are often about ordinary people struggling to make things work in a strange and even chaotic world. These jokes give a jolt, remind people of both the joy and anger in life, and suddenly they laugh.

There are hundreds of websites entirely dedicated to jokes. The key is to know how to adapt a joke to serve your current circumstances. This is touched on briefly in Secret 3, *Master public speaking*. You need to give a brief introduction that connects the joke with your present situation. This makes the joke more relevant and, somehow as a result, much funnier.

However, always tell jokes that any member of a family – old or young – can hear without embarrassment. This ensures their safety for work situations. Jokes about minorities of any kind, body parts or functions, or those that are gender biased or ridicule other people may raise a laugh, but this kind of joke also makes you look insensitive, desperate, sad or needy. Wholesome jokes are just funnier as well. In fact, your good intention in telling a joke will add value and make people like you even if they don't like the joke.

LOOK ON THE BRIGHT SIDE OF LIFE

Some people are born with a positive attitude. Others need to learn it. However it is acquired, people with a sunny disposition are great company. As an example, and this is a true story, a man arrives home at the start of a terrible economic downturn and, smiling, tells his family, 'I've lost my job. Now we have a chance to start a business – something the whole family can do together. Isn't it wonderful?'

He is actually an intelligent and well-educated man who realizes they are in for tough times, but events in his life always delight him. However, on this occasion he is in for a further surprise because during dinner he receives a phone call. An old friend, now at another company, has just heard that he has been let go and offers him a job – at a much larger salary. This kind of positive person is always in demand, always has options. Later he apologizes to his family: 'We'll have to have a regular income after all.'

So if you don't already look on the bright side of life, it's time to learn. First, it's important to face negative thoughts and reactions. Never ignore them or pretend you feel happy when you feel bad about an event. This makes you a phoney, not an optimist. Let your feelings sink in and experience that sudden stomach drop that happens at bad news. Then exercise your mind and think of why it's 100 per cent great that this event is happening at this time. 'Wow! I've just had bad news! Amazing.'

If you've never done this before, it will be hard – but try. Shift your thoughts for a moment away from being afraid or angry or upset. If you can't at first, go for a run, have some exercise, drink a cup of tea, or eat some cake – whatever it is you do to take your thoughts from very upsetting situations. You need to do this because the first step to being a sunny and positive person is having the skill to identify what is really and truly good about the worst possible situation. This is a mental process, not an emotional one. Positive people are guided by thoughts, not feelings.

Furthermore

The more you identify the good in the bad and the more frequently you do this, the better you will be at looking at the bright side of life. It will become your instinctive reaction, even if it is very difficult to learn at first. As it becomes more instinctive, you will be amazed at the doors that open to you and the interesting people you will meet.

ENJOY YOUR LIFE

You can lose your sense of humour; even forget you ever had one. Stress, overwork, illness or sadness of any kind can take over your life. It happens gradually. You may notice the change only after feeling impatient when your colleagues burst out laughing. In the past you'd have joined them to ask what's so funny. Instead, you retreat into more work. You may even feel angry that they are making so much noise.

Unhappy events can overtake you until you feel as if you've never laughed before and may never again. This may sound like an exaggeration, but it can happen to anyone. The solution is to ensure that you find time in your life to relax. Avoid filling your life with meaningless events or doing more than your health can carry.

The ability to laugh is a treasure. This strategy is to warn you that it can be lost if you fail to maintain balance in your life. But humour can be found again. Watch three silly movies in a row with people you care about. Play music and dance about the room even if your legs feel like lead, or call someone worse off than you are and talk until you raise them in a hearty laugh. Repeat until your sense of humour is back.

Putting it all together

Laughter offers great health benefits. It boosts the immune system, lowers blood pressure and cuts stress. It is a way to reach out and make friends. Every person in every nation in the world knows how to laugh. Although they may well laugh at different things, they will understand when you are laughing.

A sense of humour keeps you sane when business or life experiences go very badly. Your humour makes it easy for people to connect with you. However, there are people who use humour to create a distance between themselves and others. They tell jokes to avoid connecting. Getting behind the armour their ersatz humour creates is almost impossible. This kind of self-defence isn't really a sense of humour at all.

In contrast, a person who looks on the bright side can make you smile as soon as they enter the room. The difference is that a sense of humour connects you with others; acting the part doesn't.

16 BUILD PEOPLE UP

'I've learned that people will forget what you said, people will forget what you did, but people will never forget how you made them feel.'
Maya Angelou

'Treat people as if they were what they ought to be, and you help them to become what they are capable of being.'
Johann Wolfgang von Goethe

'Whenever you are about to find fault with someone, ask yourself the following question: What fault of mine most nearly resembles the one I am about to criticize?'
Marcus Aurelius

'A good leader inspires people to have confidence in the leader; a great leader inspires people to have confidence in themselves.'
Eleanor Roosevelt

'Keep away from people who try to belittle your ambitions. Small people always do that, but the really great make you feel that you, too, can become great.'
Mark Twain

One of a leader's more satisfying jobs is encouraging younger people to grow in skill and confidence. The young person's starting point doesn't matter. The goal is always to help them find the next step. Here is a conversation between a boss and a recently hired graduate.

'I looked for your name today on the list of applications for the certification test. Did you know that the deadline is noon today?'

'Me? My name?'

'Yes, your name. Did you use an alias?"

'Ah, no. Ah, no. I didn't use any name. I didn't register.'

'Well, the rules require that you register to take the test. It's only a short form and there's no cost.'

'Um. Ah. A short form? Then I'd have to take the test.'

'That's the idea. The company pays for your travel. All you do is take the test. Later, you learn your results.'

'Yuh, [*looking startled*] but maybe I'll fail.'

'Is that really so likely? Your work is rather good.'

'But I could get nervous. I could fail. I really could.'

'Well, I've seen your CV and you don't tend to fail.'

[*Long pause*] 'You know, I really haven't thought about taking the test so soon.'

'Good. Now you have. Now you will. See yourself as someone who takes a test just to see what happens. Just to learn how it feels. I'll put a note in your file that you're doing this for practice and that I advised it.'

[*Grinning*] 'Oh! OK. Thanks. That's great. It's almost noon, I better get going.'

This approach works when there's already a positive relationship between a boss and an employee. The more junior person has to believe that the boss wants him or her to succeed. It's a gentle nudge that shows respect for ability and awareness that the person can do more.

ENCOURAGE GROWTH AT WORK

This conversation is an example of drawing out the best from people who may have had little encouragement in the past. You may sense they have potential and can see they work hard, but they don't test their abilities fully and seem unaware of the opportunities available to them. Maybe no one has ever believed in them. If you assume – or at least appear to assume – that they will rise to the occasion, they will act like hungry fish and jump for the bait.

A direct approach, such as 'Why don't you take the certification test? You may get a pass,' risks an answer of 'No thanks.' Instead, assume that they are taking the test. At the very least it will be a positive surprise that you asked, and they will see themselves in a different light. Confidence in a person's potential can have a very powerful and lasting effect.

Of course, the assumption has to match abilities. The purpose is to support growth and so expectations have to be realistic. The boss in this example made it clear that it was OK to take the test for practice and that it would cost the younger person nothing in terms of travel costs and reputation. By minimizing the risk, the boss made it easier for the graduate to say yes.

ENCOURAGE DISCOVERY OF STRENGTHS AND WEAKNESSES

It's rewarding to see a colleague gain confidence and increase their self-belief because you assume they can grow. But a more direct approach is better for people who already have a fair idea of their abilities. The most straightforward way is to focus on their strengths and weaknesses with the goal of their building one and managing the other.

You should try this on yourself first, so that you know what you're asking of other people. Later, you can ask your colleagues to do the same. Study your own past performance to identify what you've done well and what needs improvement.

- **What are your strengths?**
  What do you do well? The answer reveals your strengths because these support your success. Strengths can be skills you've acquired or qualities you already possess or have developed. However, it's difficult to assess your own achievements, and so it's a good idea to use external measures, such as promotion, awards or positive remarks in a performance review.

- **What are your weaknesses?**
  Everyone has weaknesses, and recognizing yours will make your life easier because it will help you plan how to manage them when you are facing a difficult challenge. People who pretend they have no weaknesses or who avoid being negative about their abilities risk not knowing their limitations when it really matters.

OPEN THE WAY TO NEW PEOPLE AND EXPERIENCE

People want recognition and to be seen in a positive way. You confirm a positive opinion about others when you introduce them to new people or encourage them to have new experiences. It helps if you belong to professional, business, expert or social networks yourself. If you don't already, now is the time to act on this idea.

Very few leaders achieve success without a support network. You may be the exception, but why test this when it works so well to have a network? You also gain influence when you share your contacts. Your connection to others in modern business is a sign of your success. It confers status in line with your most important contacts. Examples of the kind of events that people value attending include:

- professional events with speakers who are leaders in their field
- invitation-only conferences where specialists discuss policy issues
- educational and technical sessions with top people contributing.

Alternatively, you can recommend that a colleague be given a chance to work on an interesting project or suggest a junior colleague offer support when someone more senior goes on leave as a way to gain experience. The idea is to look for opportunities that will challenge and inspire your colleagues. They will be very grateful and in future may return the favour.

Putting it all together

Building people up may not be part of your job description, but it is a very satisfying experience and can make your own work easier. You are indirectly preparing your colleagues for delegation and the assumption of more complex tasks. They need greater confidence for this and your encouragement gives them the opportunity to gain it. In the process you learn more about yourself.

A key aspect of this secret is that you're offering help without being asked. In one way this is kindness, but in another it's commercially smart behaviour. With one gesture you cement a relationship with a colleague who will be grateful to you for the effort you made. You add to your own network as well, not only including the person you support but also adding all the people he or she supports into the future.

17 BE VISIBLE AND HAVE PRESENCE

'Nothing is a greater impediment to being on good terms with others than being ill at ease with yourself.'
Honoré de Balzac

'Appearances matter – and remember to smile.'
Nelson Mandela

'I'm big. It's the pictures that got small.'
Norma Desmond in Sunset Boulevard

'There can be no power without mystery. There must always be a something which others cannot altogether fathom, which puzzles them, stirs them, and rivets their attention.'
Charles de Gaulle

'Leaders must wake people out of inertia. They must get people excited about something they've never seen before, something that does not yet exist.'
Rosabeth Moss Kanter

People know when leaders with presence enter the room. Without saying a word, they signal that they've arrived and everyone else raises their game. Even quiet and easy-going leaders, who encourage others to take centre stage, can have this kind of presence. It gives them instant recognition as a person with authority. Presence is based on respect and a work history that creates a great reputation.

One way to develop this is to be willing to look for solutions that meet widespread needs and solve complex problems that support a variety of interests. Another is to be aware of what colleagues need, accept their priorities, and respect their ideas. A leader with a reputation for acting wisely, caring about other people's interests, and being accountable has strength of character and this is at the core of presence. The more this develops, the greater the presence will be.

Presence usually grows gradually and strengthens as relationships develop. The first step to nurturing this growth is simple: pay close attention to what people say and watch what they do. Learn about other people's doubts, concerns, daily ups and downs and, from this, gain an idea about their priorities. A leader needs to accept and recognize other people's presence. There is a direct link between understanding and sympathizing with others and being appreciated for this and respected as a result.

Eye contact is essential to communicate presence. This means a steady gaze but not staring. It's a softened sort of watching as another person speaks. Attentive listening yields a big reward because it makes other people want to listen in return. People can't help it. Giving full attention gets full attention in a virtuous circle.

Being visible and having presence turns a good leader into an effective role model, as well as a connector, and a person who brings others together as a channel for information exchange. It's motivating for team members to have a boss who is admired for all the right reasons. They are more collaborative as a result because their leader can be counted on to maintain high standards of behaviour.

STUDY YOUR IMAGE

The word 'image' calls to mind the world of PR agencies and political spin-doctors, but everyone has an image. In fact, everyone has three of them. They are:

- how you see yourself – your self-image
- how other people see you – your perceived image
- a mix of how you and other people see you – your realistic image.

It's a good idea for leaders to work towards the third option because it's the best way to improve performance and learn what effect they have on other people. Unfortunately, some people become locked in a rigid self-image and lose the ability to listen to feedback from other people.

This can begin innocently enough by deciding that, in a changing world, they at least can stay true to their ideals. Although in principle this is a good thing, it can also create a rigid way of life: standing still while the world changes. Further, it inhibits growth and an ability to adapt to situations as necessary.

Your self-image needs constant reviewing and a good way to do this is to ask people how they see you. There can be a gap between how you see yourself and how you are seen. Although other people may be wrong, you at least have a starting point to take a good look at yourself. As a leader, your job is to inspire confidence, and if you have an image that fails to do this, you need to take immediate action.

DECIDE HOW YOU CAN IMPROVE

Presence needs to be based on a realistic image, so your first job is to discover how other people see you. You also need to know your strengths and weaknesses, your goals and your personal values. All of this helps you to begin improving your image. A realistic image gets you noticed for positive reasons, and anything less than realism runs the risk of your thinking you are admired and valued as a leader when you are not.

Wanting to learn how other people see you is far from being vain or superficial. It is a chance to see yourself from different perspectives and think about how your actions could be interpreted as well as misinterpreted. This information helps you adjust your behaviour in a way that strengthens your relationships. Ask yourself the following questions:

- Do I listen and am I responsive to what other people say?
- Are my ideas well received?
- Are the solutions I offer considered effective?
- Do I encourage other people?
- Do my colleagues understand and support me?

If you answered yes to all of these questions, then you are likely to be visible for all the right reasons. If you answered no to more than one question or you were unsure of your answer, you need to get to work.

DEVELOP YOUR PERSONAL BRAND

There's freedom in knowing what kind of impression you make on other people, or at least in having a better idea. For example, you may discover that your reputation for effective leadership isn't as strong as it once was. Colleagues who knew you well may have transferred to other areas or left the firm, a family illness may have kept you out of circulation, or your organization may have merged with another and you now work with strangers.

These kinds of change can be positive because a new situation allows you to express yourself in new ways. On a superficial level, it's new clothes and a haircut and possibly a different place to go for lunch, but, in a deeper way, you may now want to acquire new skills and discard old routines.

Here are some ideas to enhance your reputation and increase your visibility:

1. Join a new professional society or become more active in your current one.
2. Arrive early to meetings and be the last one to leave the room, making sure that you say hello to everyone there.
3. Say thank you to everyone and smile in the same way and with the same degree of warmth, whether they are the most junior of new employees or the top person.
4. Know your own values and make it clear that you base your decisions on these.

Putting it all together

All past success, hard work and support for other people gets bundled into presence. It adds to a leader's reputation for being a positive force and a benefit to the team. Having presence certainly saves time. Instead of having to convince colleagues to listen to your ideas or take your solutions seriously, they give their support as a natural consequence of being asked.

A known and respected figure receives other people's trust without having to work for it. Of course, being a highly visible leader can also be a burden. It's impossible to blend into the crowd and even social occasions can create a fishbowl effect. Genuinely modest leaders may cringe at this. They don't want to be admired or made the centre of attention.

But developing presence will, in the long run, make your life easier, and it is neither Hollywood nor fakery to work on this. Visibility and presence create credibility and remove the necessity to prove yourself again and again. Over time, this is energy saving and frees you further to encourage your colleagues to develop presence for themselves.

18 DISRUPT THE STATUS QUO

'I'm not interested in preserving the status quo; I want to overthrow it.'
Niccolò Machiavelli

'Status quo, you know, is Latin for "the mess we're in".'
Ronald Reagan

'Any business today that embraces the status quo as an operating principle is going to be on a death march.'
Howard Schultz

'I've never been very cookie cutter. If I choose something different from the status quo, it's my responsibility and my choice to live my life that way.'
Sara Ramirez

'New forms of media – first movies, then television, talk radio and now the Internet – tend to challenge traditional codes of conduct. They flout convention, shake up the status quo and sometimes provoke outrage.'
Willow Bay

Status quo is a Latin phrase loosely translated as 'the existing state of affairs' or 'the way things are'. Those who support the status quo want everything to stay the same. They argue in favour of the status quo because they believe it creates stability, and that change is disruptive and harmful. Critics of the status quo claim its lovers only want it because they benefit from keeping things as they are. They grow rich from the status quo.

Business writers in recent years actively advise in favour of disrupting the status quo. This idea may seem strange to those fighting just to keep their businesses afloat, never mind disrupting it on purpose, but there is a great deal of value in the idea. It's always good to avoid complacency and not to assume that what worked in the past will work again in the future.

Disrupting the status quo means inviting new solutions and resisting the urge to tell those with innovative ideas to stop wasting time. Disruption like this is certainly doable when managed properly, and can also be a saviour to the business. It works as long as there are systems in place to capture, explore and test new ideas while the rest of the business maintains the status quo and its stability. Disruption works well when new ideas are integrated seamlessly so that they refresh the business.

About 30 years ago, a business writer advised managers to throw their photocopiers out of the window – symbolically, of course. His idea was to energize a business entirely by discarding old routines. Those who tried this found it too disruptive, and almost all the examples of highly successful companies that this leader offered in his books have now long since gone out of business or been taken over. The secret is using the best features of disruption and escaping the worst.

One *best* feature is having a workforce of empowered, talented and skilful people who take the initiative and solve problems. The emphasis is on the creativity that can arise from disruption. A *worst* feature would be a leadership style that creates change for its own sake. These leaders commit resources on a gamble, assuming that a new IT system will work without testing it first, or that money spent on an expansion project will justify itself without showing good numbers in advance.

ENCOURAGE EVERYONE TO ASK CHALLENGING QUESTIONS

There's a cartoon showing a man standing at a boardroom table waving his arms and saying to his smiling colleagues, 'We need to innovate! Buck the status quo! Blaze a new trail! Here's how everyone else is doing it.' His message is to stay safely behind the others. This can be a good strategy when wisely employed, but it's not innovation. It doesn't challenge the status quo.

Innovation means taking risks and encouraging colleagues to challenge ideas. People committed only to following are more likely to be risk-averse and so are unlikely to enjoy confrontation or debate. Following is a good way to keep what is already there. It also allows doubling back and avoiding failure if anyone in front gets into trouble.

Asking creative and challenging questions needs to be part of the daily routine. This makes challenging the status quo – the way things are always done – a natural element of the business. The result is that innovation also becomes a way of life, and rocking the boat is a positive thing because the new ideas that emerge are so good for the business. In this instance, disruption ironically becomes the status quo.

Creative and challenging questions put the focus on the problem that needs to be solved as well as on discovering whether it is the right problem to be solved. This requires curiosity and a willingness to ask why things are done the way they are. It means questioning assumptions that are made about the business. Anyone should be able to ask anyone else why the business does what it does in the way it does.

CHALLENGE THE STATUS QUO

Dr Clark Kerr, economist and a president of the University of California until 1967, said, 'The status quo is the only solution that cannot be vetoed.' This is because, by definition, the status quo is already in place and what the majority has chosen to have is its normal. The status quo is the starting point, and to make any change from it takes a lot of energy to get things moving. Those who benefit from an existing situation will resist all ideas for change. This is a problem because people who really want change are going to push for it, and may be willing to create an explosion if that's what it takes to destroy the status quo.

In Dr Kerr's case, his presidency of a major American university occurred during a time of massive student protests about war, civil and gender rights. His campus was ready to explode at any time. He believed that the right solution was to listen to what his students had to say and to resist overreacting to their protests. He was right, and doing a good job. However, government officials – committed to the status quo – insisted that he have demonstrating students arrested and expelled, an action guaranteed to cause the explosion he wanted to avoid. When he refused to do this, he was fired.

There's a lesson here for leaders who want to change the status quo but face powerful opposition. Be careful even when you are right. Those who benefit from keeping things as they are will not let go easily. You can convince them to change only if you remove the threat of their losing face and assure them that there is something in the pot for them if they change. This means that you need to find out what will benefit a 'status quo-er' and then sell them change.

MAKE DISRUPTION WORK FOR YOU

Encouraging disruption, as a pilot project for major change, is a way to innovate, monitor and evaluate progress. It's a way to get the benefits of revolution without the mess. This is change management and it can be followed in four stages. These are:

1. **Identify what needs to change:** set a goal and define what success will look like. This gives you an initial or trial goal for disruption.
2. **Explore the context:** see how the goal for change fits into the organization as a whole. You may have identified the wrong goal or a goal that isn't exactly right. Analyse what impact your goal will have on existing systems to see whether change needs to go deeper or wider in the organization.
3. **Revise and make plans:** amend the goal as needed and make plans to execute it. This is where you adapt the goal to meet actual, organizational needs that you've identified. Then you make plans to make the goal a reality.
4. **Evaluate the goal** against the criteria for success you identified in the first stage. This is important because, if the change hasn't achieved what you want, you'll need to adjust your plans and try again. This last stage is the one that is most often ignored.

If you follow a plan for change and ring-fence the disruption it causes, you can have the status quo as well as innovation.

Putting it all together

This secret suggests you stay open to change and be willing to renew and revise former systems. You also need to make a commitment to disruption and change when necessary. This means exploring in depth what doesn't work so that you can transform the way you do business. Although major change is challenging and time consuming, it's necessary to future-proof your business.

People-management skills are essential when leading major change. The best employees will leave if you make them too uncomfortable or keep them in the dark about the reasons for change. You can shake things up and bring talented people along with you if you communicate effectively and show that disruption is necessary.

You also need to be aware that, when change threatens those with an interest in keeping everything as it is, they won't give up their position easily. Your competence and experience won't protect you if you're perceived as the enemy of order, stability and the status quo. In fact, you will be a ready-made target. Avoid this by ensuring that you have a critical mass of support for any disruption you need to create. Be patient and work to bring people along with you. It will save time in the long run.

19 EARN PEOPLE'S TRUST

'Trust yourself. Create the kind of self that you will be happy to live with all your life. Make the most of yourself by fanning the tiny, inner sparks of possibility into flames of achievement.'
Golda Meir

'Trust is the glue of life. It's the most essential ingredient in effective communication. It's the foundational principle that holds all relationships.'
Stephen Covey

'The trust of the innocent is the liar's most useful tool.'
Stephen King

'It is better to suffer wrong than to do it, and happier to be sometimes cheated than not to trust.'
Samuel Johnson

'Trust everybody, but cut the cards.'
Finley Peter Dunne

Trust marks the beginning and end of relationships, although some relationships exist in a halfway zone with never enough push towards trust and never enough cause to mistrust. Colleagues, associates and acquaintances may all fit into that category. The move to friendship and a trusted working relationship happens only after deciding how trustworthy a person is. This makes trust building an essential skill for everyone, particularly leaders, because they need to have strong relationships based on trust. Otherwise, they will never gain either influence or credibility.

What is trust? Its definition varies according to context. It can refer to the trust between a person and an organization, between two individuals, or trust in the legal sense. In general, trust is the belief that a person or an organization is reliable, truthful and capable of delivering and keeping promises. Three experts on the topic of trust, David Maister, Charles Green and Robert Galford, wrote a book called *The Trusted Advisor* (2000), in which they identify four criteria for trust. These are credibility, reliability, interpersonal connection and self-interest.

- **Credibility** (C) is a person's experience, skills, qualities and credentials – objective evidence that they are fit for purpose.
- **Reliability** (R) is consistent and regular behaviour demonstrating that a person will do what they promised on time and in the way they promised.
- **Interpersonal connection** (I) is knowledge about another person that leads to a feeling of connection, bonding and shared understanding.
- **Self-interest** (S) is the degree to which a person thinks only of his or her own interests to the detriment of other people – in other words their degree of egotism.

The authors then made an equation they call the trust equation. It looks like this:

$$\frac{C + R + I}{S} = \text{Trust}$$

Their idea is to decide a score subjectively for each item of the equation from 1 to 10, then add these numbers together. This total number – C, R and I – creates a suggestion for trustworthiness. However, the person's willingness to take advantage of other people or to serve themselves unfairly (S) is also included in the equation. Leaders with high scores for C, R and I can still receive a low overall trust score if they have a high score for self-interest.

MANAGE YOUR CREDIBILITY

Do you know whether your colleagues see you as credible? Any doubts they feel will stop them trusting you and lower your ability to lead. Here's a checklist to start exploring how people see you.

1. Do you have the credentials to do your job, such as certifications, skills and experience? ☐
2. Are these credentials widely known? ☐
3. Are you on friendly terms with bosses above you? ☐
4. Did you become friendly with them after you started your current job? ☐
5. Do your colleagues believe you earned the right to have your job? ☐

If you answered yes to all of these questions, it is likely that you have credibility. If you answered no to one or two, you may have to convince people that you are fit to do your job. If you answered no to three, you may well be held in some suspicion. If you answered no to four or five questions, it is likely that your colleagues question your skills and your ability to lead in your job. They may still trust you if you are strong in reliability and they feel some connection to you, but they may also hold back their belief in you.

This may seem unfair, even very unfair, but perception, already discussed (in Secret 6, *See the person not the stereotype*), is shaped by past experience and mental habit and happens unconsciously. Your colleagues may not fully know why they hold back, but they do anyway. Your task is to make it clear indirectly and subtly that you are fully qualified to do your job.

MANAGE YOUR RELIABILITY

You also need to think about how reliable you appear to your colleagues. This can seem ridiculous to a reliable person, but it's a matter of perception, point of view and interpretation. It's worth taking a few minutes to think about how reliable you *may* or *may not* appear to be. Here is a checklist:

1. Are there procedures everyone follows to complete work and share projects? ☐
2. Can you meet your commitments 90 per cent of the time? ☐
3. Do you take time to explain when you do not meet your commitments? ☐

4. Is it normal for everyone to openly discuss the causes of
failed commitments? ☐

5. Is blame avoided in the search to improve procedures
and meet commitments? ☐

Sometimes a lack of systems causes failed commitments and
seeming unreliability. It will help you and your colleagues if
procedures are in place to support getting work done. As for
scoring yourself, if you answered yes to all the above questions,
your colleagues will believe you are reliable. If you answered
no to three, it's likely that they don't really count on you. If you
answered no to four or five, you can assume that they don't think
you are reliable at all. Good procedures, however, can make
everyone more accountable and more reliable.

ASSESS YOUR CONNECTIONS AND SELF-INTEREST

A good way to improve your trust score is to get to know your
colleagues better, and be more open about yourself as well.
This doesn't mean that you have to become friends, spend time
outside work together, or even talk about personal issues. It
means asking how they are getting along with current work and
listening to the answer.

Encourage discussion of doubts and concerns, and also share
your own. This allows an understanding of each other's
preferences, strengths and weaknesses to grow. The end result
is an increased sense of teamwork and improved relationships.
Trust can grow only when people feel a connection to one
another.

You can also manage your self-interest. Small gestures, like
pouring coffee for other people before you take your own cup,
make a difference to how you are perceived. It sends a message
that you are part of the group, and are unlikely to be the one
who eats all the biscuits. If you have an aggressive style or are
abrupt in the way you speak, you need to make extra effort to
show fairness and honesty in your dealings. This will reassure
people that you're one of the team.

Putting it all together

The trust equation can help you to evaluate who is trustworthy and who isn't. The four variables give reference points for looking at someone's behaviour when meeting for the first time. Gut reaction may give you a sign, and then the trust equation allows you to examine why you had that reaction. It can also help build bridges when people are from different cultures or backgrounds and lack common ground.

Without a common background or shared point of view, even a person with high credibility and reliability and low self-interest can find it difficult to be accepted and understood. Gestures, language and facial expressions can have different meanings. Only spending time working together, with increased familiarity, eventually creates understanding and then trust.

What the trust equation doesn't offer is advice about when to give a second chance to someone who's lost your trust. The loss can actually seem worse if someone has always been reliable and has high credibility. It can also be very hard to forgive if you have a strong connection with the person. Secret 37, *Give people a second chance*, addresses this.

20 NEGOTIATE LASTING SOLUTIONS

'If you come to a negotiation table saying you have the final truth, that you know nothing but the truth and that is final, you will get nothing.'
Harri Holkeri

'You have to persuade yourself that you absolutely don't care what happens. If you don't care, you've won.'
Felix Dennis

'Leadership has a harder job to do than just choose sides. It must bring sides together.'
Jesse Jackson

'No is always an easier stand than yes.'
Rosabeth Moss Kanter

'My father said:"You must never try to make all the money that's in a deal. Let the other fellow make some money too, because if you have a reputation for always making all the money, you won't have many deals."'
J. Paul Getty

Anyone can make a fast trade or create a quick fix and, in the short term, dealers who do this can look very successful. When they boast about winning by beating someone down, they sound forceful and in charge. However, there are two critically important follow-on questions: do their deals last and will the people they beat ever deal with them again?

For example, the boss who denies an employee a promised pay rise loses willing co-operation in future. The salesperson who uses tricks to make a sale risks a future complaint and return of the goods. The banker who bends the rules ends up in jail. Short-term gains for these dealers mean long-term losses.

By contrast, those negotiators who work with their opposition, not against it, are able to make agreements fit for purpose that last a lifetime. Their initial hard work and determined fairness pay off because they rarely have to revisit terms. This saves time and energy that they can then use to make their next successful deal.

More than 30 years ago two Harvard professors, Roger Fisher and William Ury, wrote a book called *Getting to Yes*, in which they described the idea of win–win. This means that, for a negotiation to last, everyone involved must benefit from a deal and feel satisfied with its terms. This doesn't mean compromise. With compromise, each person gives something up in order to find agreement. There's a risk that later they may regret their flexibility and decide that their sacrifice was greater than the other person's. The Ury and Fisher method means finding a new solution based on needs, priorities and interests. They then identify a range of options to serve them.

These dealers avoid giving things up because they find good, wholesome alternatives and new ways of looking at the deal that will serve all the parties. This is extremely difficult because dealers using this method need to identify their own essential needs as well as learn about everyone else's. This adds another layer of activity to an already time-pressured situation, but it is as necessary as studying the financial data or conducting additional pre-deal research.

RECOGNIZE THE DIFFERENCE BETWEEN WANTS AND NEEDS

Babies are hardwired to signal their needs in order to survive. They need food, warmth, shelter and affection. When they get these basics, they move into the world of choice and preference. In this world, what they want can be far in excess of what they actually need. Having lots of choice can blur the line between wants and needs and result in chasing a fad idea or fashion as if life itself depends upon getting it. Self-awareness helps, of course, as does regularly asking whether all the people and things in life are really there because they are necessities.

But it's also more complicated than this because wants become habits over time and these habits are hard to break. We must also consider the wants of other people who have a legitimate claim on time, attention and resources. Relationship can turn other people's wants into needs you feel responsible for fulfilling.

Salespeople have to juggle the 'want or need' issue when meeting weekly sales targets. They're under pressure to meet these or lose their jobs. However, they have a choice about how to do this. One option is to build a network of satisfied customers who send them referrals and also return to buy more. This is a long-term solution that takes patience to create. It also means resisting the temptation to trick a customer into a big sale in order to achieve a sales target.

KNOW YOUR LIMITS AND GUESS THE OTHER SIDE'S

Before any negotiation, you need to decide what would make you walk away from the deal. This refers to the financial terms, the treatment you receive from the opposition, potential disruption to your future plans, and other issues. To learn about this, you need to explore your desired end result from the deal, and also consider the expectations of anyone you represent, such as colleagues, partners or investors.

Here is a suggested procedure that you can use:

1. Make a list of all your expectations, both yours and those of other people.
2. Circle any item on this list that you absolutely must have included in the deal.
3. Consider whether the circled items are wants or genuine needs.
4. If you decide that any items are wants, not needs, then identify possible substitutes.

5. Give serious thought to what underlies these wants. Getting to the bottom of wants makes it easier to find substitutes to serve a genuine need.
6. Identify substitutes.

Knowing your limits prepares you for dealing with tough or bullying negotiators, or dealmakers who offer to 'sweeten the deal' with add-ons you don't really need or even want. A successful deal meets your needs, and any substitutes have to meet these needs as well. If you cannot get anywhere with this, then you have to walk away. However, you also need to consider in advance what would make the other side walk away from you. This means identifying their limits and their needs.

MAKE FRIENDS AND FORM ALLIANCES

Negotiators who practise win–win are often called naive. Believers in win–lose think that looking for options that benefit both sides is a weakness, and deals that serve everyone's interests are a waste of time. Their objective is to take advantage of any weakness they can discover. These dealmakers describe this as acting in their self-interest, but in this they are entirely wrong.

Truly acting in self-interest leads to increased security, better long-term relationships and healthy prosperity. Intimidation, threats and mental games – all techniques of win–lose negotiators – create unrest, a bad reputation and the potential that someone somewhere will return for revenge. This is not self-interest. It's a recipe for losing in the long term.

Research has shown that that negotiators who use a win–win method over time are far more successful than those who are pushy and forceful. This is because win–winners make friends who offer their support when it's needed. Win–winners are a network – an alliance of members that can close ranks when under attack.

Long-term success is enabled by the kind of healthy relationships you build by creating win–win situations.

Putting it all together

Problem solvers and decision-makers get long-term results with win–win negotiation. Although it can be tempting to push a deal through or force an issue, this behaviour comes at a cost. Today's actions cast a shadow over the future.

An updated version of the Ury and Fisher method is called the Mutual Gains Approach. Its developer, Professor Lawrence Susskind, offers four steps:

1. **Preparation:** identify your limits and think of alternatives to obvious solutions.
2. **Value creation:** ask 'What if?' and brainstorm new solutions with your opposition.
3. **Value distribution:** decide on objective criteria that will create win–win.
4. **Follow-through:** think what can go wrong and prepare for this.

21 LIVE WITH UNCERTAINTY

*'Uncertainty and expectation are the joys of life.
Security is an insipid thing.'*
William Congreve

'There is no such uncertainty as a sure thing.'
Robert Burns

*'The only thing that makes life possible is permanent,
intolerable uncertainty; not knowing what comes next.'*
Ursula K. Le Guin

*'The quest for certainty blocks the search for meaning.
Uncertainty is the very condition to impel man
to unfold his powers.'*
Erich Fromm

*'We sail within a vast sphere, ever drifting in uncertainty,
driven from end to end.'*
Blaise Pascal

The economist Frank Knight said that uncertainty should not
be confused with risk. This is because methods exist to assess,
and even measure, risk but nothing helps guide the degree of
uncertainty that may lie ahead. Estimation is possible, but it
depends on a process of elimination rather than measurement.
Professor Knight said, 'You cannot be certain about uncertainty.'

Much of life is uncertain, although people live as if they know
what is going to happen next. Of course no one does, but
living normally requires pretending that plans made today will
unfold as intended tomorrow. It's crucial for leaders to continue
managing effectively even when they are entirely uncertain about
the future. Decisions must be made and carried out because, after
all, everyone is watching.

But there are ways that leaders can manage uncertainty. These include creating a trend line based on past performance, looking for patterns in current information, or just making a guess. However, this secret's main tip is that leaders succeed in times of uncertainty by accepting the situation and having the humility to realize that sometimes they are simply unsure. This small act of self-awareness prepares them to respond more quickly with alternative solutions if their best guesses prove to be wrong.

The alternative is the leader as gambler, who puts every resource into one option without a backup plan or support system available in case the gamble is lost. Experienced leaders know better than this and they develop several scenarios when making major decisions, drawing on advice from experts and other experienced people. This approach helps them to stay light on their feet and move quickly to change their plans as necessary.

Recognizing potential difficulties makes success more likely. It helps to look for and study known variables.

1. First, identify potential sources of uncertainty such as the weather, changes in personnel, sudden data loss or acquisition of a mass of new information.
2. After listing as many of these as possible, identify further issues or actions that can't be controlled or that could change suddenly.
3. Finally, produce stories about the future, which include mixtures of these variables in ways that identify what might go wrong.

BE ADAPTABLE AND KEEP AN OPEN MIND

It's rare for a new venture to go exactly as planned. Being adaptable helps you stay in control of your own reactions. Everyone looks to the leader for stability, so when you react calmly to disrupted plans, being cool-headed becomes the standard that others will then aspire to reach.

Being able to say 'We're wrong; let's fix this' takes both humility and courage, and the intelligence to realize that the initial solution was incorrect. Planning in highly uncertain situations requires monitoring what you do, as you do it, and always being prepared for the unexpected. This keeps you flexible enough to alter your course as necessary.

Staying calm also allows you to avoid rushing. At times, you will have no information about what is coming next or which reaction may be correct. You'll have pieces of a complicated puzzle and not know where the pieces go or which ones are most important. An open mind allows you to wait before taking action. The more crucial the outcome, the greater will be the need to look at evidence as it comes in before deciding what to do.

Furthermore
Uncertainty is uncomfortable for everyone, but even more so for leaders. So much depends on getting it right, but you may not know what is right and cannot decide what to do until you have a direction. You may as well be at the helm of a mini-submarine in the deepest, darkest part of the ocean. You're ready to deal with whatever is out there, but you need to see what it is before you can.

MAKE FLEXIBLE PLANS BUT STUDY OLD OUTCOMES

Once you've accepted that uncertainty is part of your life as a leader, you'll know that your plans can fall apart without warning. But you can still plan for the future by figuring out what parts of your plans will be most likely to need revision. You can also prepare by studying what others have done in the past in similar circumstances.

Once again, humility is the main quality needed so that you're ready to copy what has worked for other people. Ask people who used to do your job about the kinds of disruption they've experienced in the past and how they responded. Learning from the past isn't a guarantee that you'll know what to do in the future, but it helps to know what reactions worked before and what didn't.

Ulysses S. Grant, Commanding General of the Union Army in the American Civil War and later an American president, had attended military college with all the other generals fighting in that war. He once said that he could often predict what the others would do because they tended to repeat their behaviour as very young men during war games in college. Although a battle is uncertain, Grant's anticipation of the others' behaviour gave him a bit of the 'known' in the unknown.

Predicting outcomes based on information is an important part of human intelligence. When this information is unavailable, the body receives stress signals from the brain as an alert to danger. This need for prediction has been called 'information craving', and it occurs when the brain feels starved of information. When this happens, the brain would rather accept poor data than have none at all. This can work against your making smart decisions.

TOLERATE UNCERTAINTY

The mathematician and historian John Finley said, 'Maturity of mind is the capacity to endure uncertainty.' Research studies have shown that people with a high tolerance for uncertainty are more rapidly promoted and show greater effectiveness than those who are less tolerant.

Another study from the Center for Creative Leadership also shows that a frequent cause of executives going off the rails is an inability to manage change and a tendency to show rigid reactions to disrupted plans. For example, some leaders stubbornly refuse to adapt when things turn out differently from what they expected. Then, when it's obvious to everyone that they made the wrong decision, their dark side emerges.

Leaders who suffer severe frustration when their plans don't work may, in some cases, take their feelings out on their colleagues. A leader who is normally positive when things go well can suddenly become hostile, angry and bullying when experiencing the prospect of failure. These are leaders who cannot handle being uncertain and refuse to accept having zero control over what happens next. Unfortunately, the victims of their bad behaviour remember it long after the uncertainty is resolved.

Putting it all together

Managing uncertainty in times of increasing complexity and rapid change makes planning very difficult, but it has to be done. There is no certain way to prepare for uncertainty. This is why this secret suggests accepting it as part of life and just living with it. This is easier if you first recognize that it's your constant companion anyway and then decide that uncertainty offers more positives than negatives.

If all events unfolded as planned, this would be a world without surprise and life would be monotonous and dull. Uncertainty means possibility and the chance to benefit from surprise. Calm and steady leaders use uncertainty to find new solutions. The main requirement is an open mind and, as mentioned before, the humility to realize that you can learn from others and you don't need to have all the answers yourself.

22 GIVE RESPECT TO GET RESPECT

'If you fail to honour your people, they will fail to honour you.'
Lao Tzu

'Rank does not confer privilege or give power. It imposes responsibility.'
Peter Drucker

'Leadership is an honour bestowed upon you, and you better be ready for it. You better be willing and able to earn the respect of those whom you are leading.'
Jackie Reses

'You can have a certain arrogance, and I think that's fine, but what you should never lose is the respect for the others.'
Steffi Graf

'When we show our respect for other living things, they respond with respect for us.'
Arapaho Indian proverb

The shop-floor machinists are staging another go-slow, and Ned Turner decides to take the long way home to think through his options. They seem few. Having risen from shop-floor machinist himself to become a supervisor, he understands his former colleagues' point of view. He also shares their current boss, Richard Tolla, who manages five other supervisors who each also supervise teams of 20 machinists.

Ned can't understand Richard's behaviour. Surely he realizes that a go-slow makes him look bad to the big bosses, and that his lack of good production numbers will be evaluated when it's time for a bonus. It's his job to ensure that those numbers are achieved and the CEO will blame him, not the machinists. Ned has explained that members of his team feel overworked, receive no thanks for their effort, and find their working conditions increasingly unpleasant and even unsafe.

Richard just cuts him off, saying that they should be grateful to have jobs. This surprised Ned at first because Richard's predecessor was good with people and ensured that they had what they needed to do a good job. By contrast, Richard is obsessed with cutting costs as a quick fix for bottom-line improvement. These days Ned never voices an opinion, shares his ideas or suggests solutions; Richard has ignored or ridiculed him too often.

But Ned listens to Richard, who tells him how unhappy he is with his own boss, the company CEO. He makes cruel remarks about Richard's weight and encourages Richard's peers to laugh at him as well and join the bear-baiting. As Ned arrives home, he decides to update his CV and get a new job by the end of the year.

His work has begun to affect his home life. The evening before, he just caught himself before making a cutting remark to his much-loved child. He fears that he has let slip other negative remarks and is determined not to allow work to spoil his home life. His lack of respect from Richard is causing him to show disrespect as well and he won't let that happen.

DECIDE WHETHER YOU WOULD FOLLOW YOU

Think about the last time you interviewed people for a job. How did you behave as an interviewer? Did you allow the applicants to answer fully, listening without interrupting them, or did you finish their sentences or look away when they began to speak? Take a few moments to think about this because it's one way to gain insight about your attitude to other people and your ability to show them respect.

A job interview is, after all, among the top ten events causing the most stress, for both applicant and interviewer. Good, bad and ugly personality traits all come out in stressful situations. If you are happy with your behaviour, in terms of showing applicants genuine consideration and respect, it is very likely that this carries into the workplace. It shows that you may be a good boss, or at least one who shows respect.

Mutual respect is essential for good relationships. It enables frank discussion and constructive criticism. It's also the basis for business growth because opportunities arise as ideas are shared and different points of view are discussed. By contrast, when there is a lack of respect, people are self-protective. They don't risk sharing their ideas because the likelihood of being ridiculed is too great. This means that there will be few, if any, innovative ideas and a resistance to change.

RESPECT YOURSELF

Self-respect is at the core of being able to respect other people. It's a virtuous circle. You respect your colleagues; they value this, and see you in a positive way as well. Here are two questions to help you decide whether you have healthy self-respect.

- **Are you able to control your impulses?**
  Have you ever realized that you were about to do something harmful to your health or happiness, and yet were unable to stop yourself? Being able to say no to an extra slice of pie or refuse that final drink are just small examples of healthy impulse control. Examples of low control include taking a holiday without having money to pay for it, shouting at the boss and losing your job, or disappointing and hurting members of your family.

- **Do you take care of your appearance, your health and your money?**
  These are all essentials to ensure that you maintain a feeling of well-being. Your appearance is a shop window that tells everyone how you feel about yourself. For example, dirty hair or hands for someone who works in an office can be a signal that something is wrong. Taking care of your health with good diet and exercise is a sign that you care about yourself. Your money is another measure of self-respect. If you are chronically overdrawn, then you need to show more respect for your own security.

Increase your self-respect by choosing to change just one behaviour each week. Avoid trying to do more because changing one habit is hard enough. If you try two or three, there's a risk of giving up. Choose one behaviour to improve either impulse control or taking care of yourself. Stay conscious of changing this behaviour all week. When you have changed, move to the next habit you want to improve.

LISTEN TO GAIN RESPECT

Stress can cause extreme reactions to innocent remarks and potentially harm your relationships. It can result in your questioning a colleague's meaning even when you've heard, but not reacted to, the same remark in the past. Stress can lead to misunderstandings, puzzled reactions and further stress, both for yourself and for your colleagues.

You can relieve stress, however, by listening to the other person and forgetting about yourself. Listening is an antidote to stress and anxiety because it takes concentration and shifts your attention fully to someone else. You may also get a positive reaction from your colleague who may also be under stress. Listening can create a virtuous circle. Allowing stress to fester leads to a negative spiral.

Listening is also an essential way to show respect. Another is to discover what interests other people, and you can find this out through casual conversation. So make time to ask how other people are getting along. Mention a current shared challenge and let your colleagues know you are interested in their work. Follow this with silence to signal your willingness to listen.

There are people who dislike making small talk or chatting because it seems a waste of time. However, in the animal kingdom a way to show kinship or respect is through mutual grooming. Making civil remarks and caring enough to listen is a form of grooming in the workplace.

If you really dislike chat, then a friendly smile while you listen to others exchanging minor bits of news is OK as well.

Putting it all together

Respectful behaviour sets a standard. It's also highly attractive socially to give way to someone older or more deserving of a better place. People seeing you behave well are then more likely to show you respect. They may even copy you. This is how shared habits develop in families and among groups of friends. Gradually, everyone adopts the same behaviour as everyone else.

Respect grows in healthy relationships as you learn more about other people and as they learn about you. It's also a way to gain insight into solving problems and meeting challenges. This requires listening with a wish to understand what's being said and learning from this. If you can imagine yourself in another person's shoes as they go about their lives, it will be easy to understand their need for your respect.

23 UNDERSTAND DIFFERENT POINTS OF VIEW

'Leadership should be born out of the understanding of the needs of those who would be affected by it.'
Marian Anderson

'Without accepting the other person's thinking, you cannot further your own interest. You need the other's help to get results.'
Harri Holkeri

'To be one, to be united is a great thing. But to respect the right to be different is maybe even greater.'
Bono

'I don't think there is any truth. There are only points of view.'
Allen Ginsberg

'When once your point of view is changed, the very thing which was so damning becomes a clue to the truth.'
Arthur Conan Doyle

There are people who push their opinions on to other people. Their point of view is the only one that counts, regardless of accuracy, new information, a well-reasoned alternative or physical evidence of any kind. They know they are right and that's that. These people are also very tiresome and limited. Obviously, there is a better way.

Recent research from Columbia University reports that military leaders, CEOs and politicians who are able to see different points of view get better problem-solving results. But they also have to be willing to act on what they learn. Although some leaders are able to navigate through difficult situations, they lack the necessary assertiveness to make the required changes based on what they learn from other people.

This research has also revealed that the most powerful leaders are less likely to recognize different points of view and believe that their ideas are the only ones that count or even exist. This could result from them having to push their opinions forward on their way to the top. Their success depended on their having a forceful and confident delivery style. Gradually, the idea that other points of view existed would disappear.

These single-idea leaders are shown in this research to be less successful than those who realize that a leader's job changes on reaching the top. To succeed, senior-level leaders need to draw ideas from colleagues and learn from what they hear. Active listening to understand new perspectives can seem weak to leaders accustomed to being in command, but failing to adopt new skills turns them into 'one-trick ponies' driven by their own views and isolated from other people.

Finally, the research suggests that leaders who accept, or at least explore, new ideas are more effective and successful, because they:

- promote an atmosphere where information is shared freely so that complex problems are solved more easily
- realize the importance of maintaining balance and integrating different ways of thinking, which leads to long-lasting, effective and robust decisions.

There's a saying that a problem shared is a problem halved. Not only is it a relief to share the burden of responsibility, but there's the added benefit of fresh ideas.

GET EVERYONE TALKING

There are two golden rules for encouraging discussion. The first is, when sharing doubts, fears, concerns or anything that requires personal disclosure, that the most powerful person in the room should speak first. This is because it's high risk for a junior person to talk about their doubts and fears in front of the boss. But if the boss goes first, this sets the tone and style that others can copy. The second rule is, when discussing factual matters and asking opinions about the usefulness of an idea, that the most junior people should go first. This avoids any parroting of the boss's opinions – because they haven't heard them yet. It also encourages everyone to express a view. The implicit message is this: if the most junior can speak up, anyone can. This enables genuine problem solving and an in-depth discussion.

An often used, but misguided, way to start a discussion is by asking, 'Any questions?' There rarely are. Presentations are so often about facts and are rarely interesting enough to produce a meaningful question. Besides, if someone does have a question, it will be related to the presenter's content. This makes it a Q&A session, not a way to generate new ideas through discussion.

The purpose of discussion should be to encourage people to share their points of view. A better method for starting a meaningful discussion is to ask those present to:

- suggest alternative or additional sources for new ideas or data collection
- identify at least one point in the presentation that needs further development
- assume that there's an error in the presentation and find it.

REACH OUT TO GROW

John Foster Dulles, a former US Secretary of State, said, 'The measure of success is not whether you have a tough problem to deal with, but whether it's the same problem you had last year.' Solving problems so that they stay solved is crucial. The alternative is wasted time and effort as well as the disappointment and loss of momentum for a project.

Drawing on team members who all have different ways of seeing the world – and therefore the problem – is ideal, but not always possible. A way to bring fresh ideas to a potentially stale situation is to use a creative problem-solving technique that requires each person to discuss the problem from the perspective of people from very different backgrounds and careers. These could include a firefighter, a circus performer, an accountant, a window cleaner or someone from a different continent or culture. The idea is to adopt that perspective as your own and see the world through different eyes. This brings diversity to the discussion because different ways of life also have varying priorities.

The more diversity that you can bring to solving a problem, the less likely it is that the solution will be stale or just another fix on what has been done before. This technique works by asking everyone at the start of a discussion to choose a point of view different from their own, and then listen to the presentation from that point of view. This method has led to new applications for old products, identification of security breaches, revised health and safety guidance, and street sign improvement, to name a few of many solutions that fresh points of view have brought to problem solving.

IMPROVE YOUR UNDERSTANDING

Knowledge, direct experience and access to the media broaden the mind and can support understanding of other people and situations. Successful leaders need this in order to reach out and connect to other people. From ensuring that you have something to chat about with strangers at a bus stop to negotiating difficult deals, understanding other people's lives and situations builds a bridge between you and them.

Here are some ways to challenge your own point of view:

- **News stories** – read newspapers and listen to or watch news programmes that support a different political party or cultural priority than your own. Even if the stories cause you to feel such fury that you grind your teeth into dust, keep going with it. This opens the way to understanding what drives the opposition. Difference is dangerous without understanding.
- **Maps** – learn the location of the places you hear about. Look for rivers and cities on a map or on a globe. Find where they

are in relation to other physical locations. This will make more enjoyable the experience of meeting new people from different places.

- **Travel** – visit places that interest you and ask a local guide to show you unusual or little-known sites. Learn how local laws and decisions are made; listen to local music; eat food you would never touch at home.
- **Commuting** – take a different route from usual and stop at a coffee shop you've never visited when on your way. At least once a week, act as if your commute to work were an excursion while on holiday. Try new ways of getting from A to B.

Putting it all together

Creative people are able to shift perspective at will. This is often the source of their inspiration, invention and art. But most people readily shift their points of view when watching a film. Identifying with the people on the screen is your entry to another world. One minute you are sitting safely in your cinema seat or on the sofa at home, and the next you are sailing on a ship at sea, or in the VIP lounge of a darkened nightclub, or hiding in an airport hangar held under siege. Each movie setting offers you an opportunity to adopt a different point of view, and the drama makes it easy for you to slip into seeing the world through the eyes of its heroes and villains.

It's only a bit more difficult to use this skill to look at the world through fresh eyes as a leader. Before an important negotiation, you can imagine what life is like for the other side. How and where do they live? What's important to them? What goes on in their everyday life? If they were characters in a film, who would play them? This kind of question opens the way to understanding their points of view.

24 LEARN FROM FAILURE

'The greatest glory in living lies not in never falling, but in rising every time we fall.'

Nelson Mandela

'Judgement comes from experience and experience comes from bad judgement.'

Simón Bolívar

'I have not failed. I've just found 10,000 ways that won't work.'

Thomas Alva Edison

'Take chances, make mistakes. That's how you grow. Pain nourishes your courage. You have to fail in order to practise being brave.'

Mary Tyler Moore

'Biologists have a word for the way that solutions emerge from failure: evolution. Often summarized as survival of the fittest, evolution is a process driven by the failure of the less fit.'

Tim Harford

'Learn from failure.' This phrase is easy to say and is so often heard after a loss or serious mistake. Of course, it's meant to ease disappointment and the frustration of losing, and for a minor failure it can help. Catchphrases are designed to encourage further action and they're usually said with good intentions. But massive loss can result in a loss of perspective as well. Hope can disappear and emotional paralysis can set in. Learning from failure in this case can feel impossible.

To avoid serious reactions to failure and also ensure learning from experience – good or bad – a project should be seen, right from the start, as part of a bigger story or as a stage in a longer process. This makes learning from failure easier because it avoids isolated thinking so that progress to a new project or venture goes more smoothly. There are inventors who actually say, 'Oh good, that failed. Now I can try doing things another way.' For them failure is both helpful and way to move forward.

It's very hard to examine failure when there's nothing else going on. A new venture allows for testing improvements. Even when a project is near its end and success is 99.99 per cent assured, it's still a good idea to think about what happens next. This means keeping one eye on the next step and one on completing the project. Make sure there is a next step and a new role is available. This is just in case the effort does fail or there are features that could have gone better; then analysis of any failure can ride on the same wave of energy that gets the new project under way.

Another essential for learning from failure is to be willing to act on improvements, even to alter things entirely to move a project forward. This can be difficult because often solutions that are similar to past attempts will seem correct. Even when a project has been team led and the whole team identifies what went wrong, members can still find it difficult to invent a new solution because they are the same people who invented the failure. Acting on improvements starts with an in-depth rethink of what went wrong.

EXPERIMENT AND SEE WHAT HAPPENS

Trial and error means a repeated and varied attempt to solve a problem until either success or the agent stops trying. It is an unsystematic method that avoids insight, theory or any organized methodology. It is therefore a good way to avoid getting stuck in a problem-solving rut because trial and error puts random ideas together without a plan or prepared sequence.

The approach could also be called guesswork and it has zero scientific rigour. It's not for the faint-hearted because there is no way to predict what happens next, and also there may be 99 failed trials before you achieve success on the 100th try. It takes an enormous amount of determination and an unwillingness to quit, but this mix-and-match approach often leads to creative solutions and allows you to work in areas where you have no knowledge at the very start.

You may have to analyse why your solution worked after the fact, because the answer emerged without any advanced planning. In this case, you are learning from success – not failure. Trial and error is also a good way to toughen up against feelings of disappointment.

Problem solving with this approach is more like practising your golf swing, playing piano scales or working a giant picture puzzle. Each trial that fails reveals new information that you can apply to the next trial. The errors are helpful and support the end result. Further benefits are fresh ideas, an ability to stretch your skill and knowledge areas. Also, you've found practical and workable solutions that are not restricted by preconceived ideas.

BOUNCE BACK FROM DEFEAT

Making a comeback requires courage, self-belief and optimism about life in general. Leaders need these qualities embedded in their DNA because their role leaves them open to failure on a regular basis. Daniel Goleman, thought leader for emotional intelligence, calls this ability to bounce back resilience. He suggests that getting up again right after being knocked over makes you resilient.

The word 'resilience' is applied to materials as well as people. Its definition is 'the ability to absorb energy when deformed, respond elastically, and return to an original shape without distortion after that energy is unloaded'. In human terms, this means that you can take a hit, absorb it without losing your sense of self, and when pressure is removed, return to your original form still expressing your unique point of view.

Nelson Mandela is a good example. His imprisonment for 30 years with humiliation on a daily basis, his eventual grant of freedom, and finally his profound ability to forgive demonstrates human resilience. His bounce-back, however, was also a personal transformation, with the pressure of his imprisonment having generated wisdom and tolerance.

There are less inspiring comebacks from sports and film stars as well as from terrible political leaders who are defeated but still return again and again. It seems that a person's character is less important than their determination, and this quality may hold the secret for developing resilience. You, too, can come back smiling and for a better reason than a television host caught shoplifting a can of tuna.

SEE FAILURE AS A GOOD THING

Seeing failure as a good thing is the secret to learning from it. However, sometimes it's easier to deny that defeat is happening even when it's obvious. It's also been said that admitting defeat can lead to taking the blame for any losses, and unfortunately this often does seem to be the case.

As highly social animals, people dislike being blamed. It feels like being made an outcast or scapegoat for the group, whether it's the family, a social circle or the team at work. So the first step to seeing failure as a good thing is to overcome the fear of being blamed and prepare to ignore it if blaming does occur. Make it your personal policy to admit to mistakes and explain how and when you will fix them. If they cannot be fixed, then describe your alternative plans.

This is crucial for your leadership. Defensive behaviour makes you look less confident. The opposite behaviour, such as ignoring your mistakes, can appear lazy and negligent. Candour and sincerity about failure presented with a positive attitude about fixing mistakes strikes a middle course.

Putting it all together

There is a definition of insanity that says it is doing the
same thing over and over again, but expecting a different
result each time. Failing to learn from failure fits that
definition of insanity. It's similar to saying, 'Oops, I just
made a mistake and now I'll repeat it.' No one wants to do
this, but it does happen. It relates to the human tendency to
create routine and find comfort in repetition, and may be
the reason people so often return to the same situations that
caused them problems in the past.

It's difficult to choose to do anything in a new way, and
learning from failure means doing just that. To join the
ranks of those who use failure as a stepping stone, it's first
necessary to throw away what's gone before in order to
build something new. Learning from failure means going
deep and analysing why things went wrong. Sometimes
there's no apparent reason for it, but it doesn't help to leave
things like that. There's always something to learn, even if
it's the decision not to get into that kind of situation again.

25 MAKE YOUR POINT AND THEN STOP TALKING

'Brevity is the soul of wit.'
William Shakespeare

'If you have nothing to say, say nothing.'
Mark Twain

'Be amusing: never tell unkind stories; above all, never tell long ones.'
Benjamin Disraeli

'It is greed to do all the talking but not to want to listen at all.'
Democritus

'Silence is a source of great strength.'
Lao Tzu

Leaders need to focus, and one way they do this is by keeping to the point when speaking. Everyone has had the experience of listening to a long presentation and wondering when the speaker will finally get to the point, even wondering whether the point has already been made long since. This is frustrating, and people who talk too much or wander endlessly around their topic undermine their own credibility.

People lose interest when ideas don't fit together, when core information is buried in tedious detail, or when the wrong kind of information is presented along with unrelated topics. Valuable data and useful ideas get hidden in the mix so that a listener may decide that it's just too much trouble to look for it. The following list shows three examples of speakers who are out of control, with suggestions for dealing with them.

- **'Me first' syndrome**
  Some leaders see their position as a free pass to share their every opinion and give unlimited direction. An antidote is to make a direct and clear request to them to allow others to speak, but this may not be possible if the talkative person is also the boss. An alternative solution is to follow up a conversation with an email, or short memo summarizing essential ideas and asking for confirmation. Another far more drastic solution is to avoid the person.

- **Expert's generosity**
  The reason for this person's compulsive talking is to inform, share, guide and educate, and very likely they have a depth of learning and wisdom that supports this. In contrast to those with 'me first' syndrome, the expert wants to be questioned and is delighted when challenged. An antidote that works well is specifying exactly what areas of knowledge need to be covered and setting a time limit, in a respectful way, for hearing the answers.

- **Random content or incoherence**
  This person is guilty of presenting too much information in a disorganized way with possible inclusion of unrelated content as well. The cause is poor judgement or lack of discipline that results in a monologue mixing opinion with fact. One antidote is to request a follow-up paper, email or memo that features the core topics in bullet-point format. It's unlikely that this will happen, but it makes a point that greater clarity is needed.

FOCUS YOUR COMMENTS AT MEETINGS

This strategy applies only if you speak regularly at meetings. If you never contribute, this is a different issue entirely. Refer instead to Secret 17, *Be visible and have presence.*

Wayne Miller, founder and CEO of an engineering company, is recognized and highly regarded as an expert in his field. Unfortunately for his staff, his encyclopedic knowledge and keen desire to educate and inform compels him to comment on every contribution made by others during meetings. Because he also often leads these meetings, no one is in a position to ask him to stop talking.

The result has been that Wayne's meetings notoriously go on for hours. His colleagues complain to one another but never to him. Wayne is so well meaning that no one wants to be petty. The result is that he never hears the complaints and therefore never realizes that he talks too much.

Wayne is an extreme example but anyone who is highly expert is at risk. To avoid talking too much in meetings, remember to:

- let other people have their say
- ask other people to give their reactions before commenting yourself
- limit yourself to one comment only; save it until the last minute and you may find that someone else raises the topic you planned to raise
- when you do speak, be brief and make one point only; if anyone wants to know more, they will ask.

USE SILENCE TO EMPHASIZE YOUR MESSAGE

Many film stars have such expressive faces that they seem to tell a story even when silent. Their thoughts, feelings and reactions are revealed through their eyes and on their face. Through their silence, you sense their thoughts and connect with them. Silence can convey as much meaning as a thousand words.

A shared silence can also create a durable connection between colleagues. Both people suddenly drawing the same conclusion with faces lighting up in an 'OMG' moment. On these occasions, there's nothing to say and so people say nothing. But it still feels as if a great deal has been said.

Not talking is also a good communication technique when you want to show you think a point that's been raised is important or you want a proposed idea to sink in and be accepted. It's effective because it gives everyone time to reflect and consider what has gone before. The result can be a more productive discussion generating better solutions. This is also called 'active listening' and it energizes meetings and empowers colleagues to take responsibility for new ideas.

DECIDE IN ADVANCE WHAT YOU WANT TO SAY

In normal conversation, we make decisions about what to say as our speaking progresses. We begin a sentence and then the next bit follows naturally as our thoughts develop. Scientists have detected only a millisecond pause when this improvisation occurs, so that thinking of what to say and saying it occur almost simultaneously.

This makes it easy to recognize when speech is rehearsed and so planning what to say is unsuitable for everyday conversation. However, you should prepare your content and structure for bigger occasions, such as speaking to a group, because this improves your coherence and clarity. The purpose of preparation is focusing your remarks and avoiding any unnecessary information, repetition or a wandering style.

It helps to decide in advance the points you want to make and then to prioritize these in an outline. This will keep you on track when you're speaking. If you run out of time, at least you know that you covered the most important points first, and came across in a natural way as you did this.

Furthermore

Outlines allow you to speak to each point and expand on it in a relaxed way. In contrast, memorized speeches seem stilted and formal. Keeping an outline in mind takes practice, but is useful if you are interrupted by a question or comment.

Putting it all together

Leaders who know how to manage the way they speak are highly respected. To ensure that you are among their number, regularly take a behaviour inventory. Ask yourself the following questions:

- In my last conversation, for what proportion of the time did I do the talking?
- Did my colleagues agree with what I said or did they challenge me?
- How often did I ask my colleagues what they thought?
- How often did I allow silence to occur?

When you prepare for a talk or leading a discussion, make a list of priority points that matches the amount of time you have for each situation. For a meeting with several people, some of whom may have a question or comment, have no more than one point for each agenda item. For short catch-up meetings that someone else requests, have no points to make. Your job is to listen to the other person's points, reflect and respond.

26 LISTEN WITH YOUR EYES AS WELL AS YOUR EARS

'The most important thing in communication is hearing what isn't said.'
Peter Drucker

'I met my grandfather just before he died, and it was the first time that I had seen Dad with a relative of his. It was interesting to see my own father as a son and the body language and alteration in attitude that comes with that, and it sort of changed our relationship for the better.'
Christian Bale

'People need realness, reality. People can sense when someone is being pretentious or fake. It's because you feel it; you see it in someone's body language.'
Afrojack (Nick van de Wall)

'Listen with your eyes for feelings.'
Stephen Covey

'Listening is not just hearing what someone tells you word for word. You have to listen with a heart. I don't want that to sound touchy-feely; it is not. It is very hard work.'
Anna Deavere Smith

On a basic level, this secret refers to making eye contact, a suggestion so important and essential that it's included in every course, book and media message available about effective communication. The eyes reveal meaning, either in support of or in conflict with what's being said aloud. Glancing away, dropping a gaze, or hiding the eyes behind dark lenses sends a non-verbal message that there is something to hide.

This may be true, but it could also mean feeling so rushed that it's easier to save a second by not looking up from the paperwork. This is a big mistake, however. Always look up and gain an understanding of how the other person reacts to the conversation. Their eyes reveal this and it's crucial for leaders to know what impact they have on others.

Eye contact is a crucial communication habit, along with watching other non-verbal communication signals. There is so much evidence about how important this is. A study from the University of California Los Angeles suggests that 93 per cent of communication effectiveness results from non-verbal signals. Another study shows that a good communication performance is 7 per cent verbal, 38 per cent quality of voice and 55 per cent non-verbal communication. Features of non-verbal communication to look for include distance, gestures and facial expressions. Understanding and interpreting this information, however, can be complicated by differences in culture, gender, age and profession.

It helps to see people as a single communication package made up of voice, eyes, hands, feet, body, face, how they stand, how they walk, and much more.

Focusing on just the spoken words loses access to the wealth of information about what people really want to say. At times, they may not know themselves what they mean or what they believe is important. An excellent listener can help them communicate, for example, by responding to their gestures as well as to their words.

It's interesting that no matter how well a dishonest person conceals the truth, there's always a signal or an incongruity in the lie's delivery that reveals that something is not quite right. This is because it takes a lot of energy to hide meaning. Some small part somewhere in the liar has to hold the mask in place. This is the chink in the armour and a sensitive reader of non-verbal communication can usually – if not always – find it.

LOOK AT DISTANCE, GESTURES AND FACIAL EXPRESSIONS

It's a good idea to assume that the other person is watching your body language as well as listening to what you say. This may not be the case, but it can help you develop or improve your awareness of how you express yourself non-verbally. Start with the three main features of non-verbal expression: distance, gestures and facial expression.

- **Distance:** Be aware when people take a step back or a step towards you. In the same way, notice your behaviour towards other people. Do you move away or towards other people? This is a distance issue and, when meeting people from different cultures and backgrounds, it's important to be sensitive to it. In the West, people who are having a casual conversation stand about half a metre apart. In Eastern societies it is often normal to stand as close as 20 centimetres apart.
- **Gestures:** This refers to arm and hand movement, swaying, head nodding, pacing and stamping. Culture, age and health all influence this communication feature. Before deciding what a gesture means, learn more about the person speaking. As for you, what gestures, if any, do you use? Ask yourself whether other people can easily understand what your gestures mean. If you suspect not, then either explain what you mean or stop using that gesture.
- **Facial expression:** This can include people who speak to you with their eyes closed and others who show their teeth in an automatic grin. They may not know they do this and what impact it has on other people. But – more importantly – do you know how you arrange your face when speaking? When you are rushed and under stress, what are you doing with your facial muscles? Are you easy to look at? Are you scary?

UNDERSTAND DIFFERENCES

Some aspects of body language result directly from culture, gender, age and profession. Body language is also acquired or learned on purpose so that it's almost impossible to read meaning into someone's actions. However, you can avoid making mistakes or misjudging people by learning more about their backgrounds.

For example, many people from Mumbai shake their heads so that they look as if they are saying no. Hand gestures can also mean very different things to those from other countries. A positive signal to one can be a rude sign to another. Silence can also mean different things: it can mean refusal to some and acceptance to others.

Learning to understand non-verbal communication opens the way to better contact with people from other backgrounds. You may have to ask people what they mean when they behave in an unexpected way, use a strange gesture, stare, blink or shudder. This is all to the good. The one thing you must avoid, however, is judging non-verbal behaviour until you really do know what it means.

NOTICE HOW PEOPLE WALK TOWARDS YOU AND AWAY

There are people who say they know everything about a person by the way they walk. However, this boast forgets that many issues can affect the way a person walks: for example, they might have sore feet, suffer from an illness, feel tired that day, have a sports injury, be very overweight, have studied dance, or be a regular in the the gym.

But you can often guess mood by the way someone approaches you, and they often reveal their reaction to what went on between you in the way they walk away. Of course, this is all guesswork, but if it helps you better understand other people then it's worth exploring. You have to look at the whole person, however, not just swinging arms and set of shoulders, not just the face, the head or the hands. The *whole person* means from the top of the head to the feet, and taking this in is harder than it sounds. Practise on yourself in the mirror. Next, practise on family or friends as they walk towards you, but also explain what you're doing in case you haven't got the knack and end up staring at them.

Next, try to guess their mood from the way they move. As you watch them, can you tell how they feel about meeting you? It helps to ask yourself how you would feel if you moved in that way. Then check and ask them how they feel. See if your guess was correct. Keep trying until you are confident that you can interpret mood.

Putting it all together

It's difficult enough to listen to what people are saying, never mind adding to this by watching non-verbal signals. But both are essential for effective communication. Salespeople are very skilled at reading non-verbal signals. They particularly watch the eyes for pupil dilation because the pupil expands in response to emotional reactions as well as to light. It's said that the eyes reveal a decision before the person fully realizes it's been made.

Eyes, gestures and face all work together to communicate. Giving attention to one over the other ignores important information. Leaders who listen with their eyes are both effective and smart because they extract meaning from both verbal and non-verbal messages. They can build on what their colleagues tell them with greater accuracy and understanding.

Communication is one of the most difficult skills that anyone can acquire, although many people take it for granted. Regular assessment of how skilled you are as a communicator will support your leadership skill as well.

27 WRITE IN A SIMPLE STYLE USING PLAIN LANGUAGE

'Good writing is like a windowpane.'
George Orwell

'The most important thing is to read as much as you can, like I did. It will give you an understanding of what makes good writing and it will enlarge your vocabulary.'
J. K. Rowling

'The writer must believe that what he is doing is the most important thing in the world. And he must hold to this illusion even when he knows it is not true.'
John Steinbeck

'It's a luxury being a writer, because all you ever think about is life.'
Amy Tan

'Not that the story need be long, but it will take a long while to make it short.'
Henry David Thoreau

Writing is another way for leaders to communicate. They need this skill to get their message across when they can't be present. Poor writing can create misunderstandings because the reader can't ask questions if any of the writing is unclear. Anything in writing has a long shelf life, so documents giving directions or reports summarizing events can be accessed long after their author has changed jobs or moved companies.

Whatever the kind of writing – whether email, blogging, letters, instructions, memos, minutes, presentations, reports or logs – it must use clear, precise and concise language. It also must be free of errors and strike a tone appropriate to the format used – for example, a friendly tone is not appropriate in minutes or memos, but is fine in a blog.

Here are three critical issues for authors of professional or business documents:

1. **Identify the result the writing should produce.** This should be the core idea or ideas that the author wants the reader to understand so that it's completely clear what should happen next. Business writing is always purpose-driven. If it doesn't fulfil its intended purpose, it's an unsuccessful piece of writing.

2. **Decide whether to explain, inform or describe.** Each of these requires a different format in business writing.
   a. *Explaining* is useful for giving directions or anything that tells someone how to do something.
   b. *Informing* is often used for memo writing, to let people know what is about to happen; or in minutes from a meeting to summarize what occurred.
   c. *Describing* is for report writing, where events need to be recorded as they actually happened.

3. **Check and recheck to ensure accuracy.** Business writing is unforgiving: not a single typo or factual inaccuracy is acceptable. Spellcheckers make this easier, but they don't guarantee accuracy, particularly of people's names or their locations. 'Autocorrect' can also make a shambles of an otherwise well-presented document. It's worth the time it takes to check that names and places are presented correctly. It reflects very badly on the writer if they do not.

CHOOSE YOUR PERSPECTIVE

Perspective in writing refers to the way you address your audience. There are three options called *first, second* and *third* person, and you can choose which one to use according to the purpose and needs of your writing.

- **First person.** With this perspective, you use the words 'I', 'me' and 'my'. It's as if you are speaking directly to your reader and it's useful when you want to personalize your writing. It's like having a conversation. Here are examples:
  - I attended the conference on 2 June and met the sales team.
  - The new results helped me understand the old report.
  - My vote about the rate changes is public knowledge.
- **Second person.** This perspective uses the words 'you', 'your' and 'yours'. It's as if you are advising or telling the reader what to do. It's good for giving directions and guidance.
  - When you go to the conference on 2 June, try to meet the sales team.
  - The new results will help you understand the old report.
  - Your vote about the rate change is public knowledge.
- **Third person.** This perspective uses 'he', him', 'his', 'she', 'her', 'hers', 'it', 'its', 'they', 'them' and 'their'. It's a good way to keep things more formal. As an author you remove yourself from the story and 'he', 'she', 'it' and 'they' take over as the main character.
  - When they went to the conference on 2 June, they met the sales team.
  - The new results will help her understand the old report.
  - His vote about the rate change is public knowledge.

WRITE CLEAR DIRECTIONS

Writing directions for other people to follow is surprisingly difficult because you need to see the task through their eyes and identify the steps they need to take. Your reader may know nothing or everything already. You need to be brief and use language that everyone understands and add descriptive words when this will help, such as:

- The green button opens the red door.
- Sound the alarm at volume 5 when the orange light goes on.

Directions are best written in the second person because you want the reader to feel actively involved and part of the process. The word 'you' makes the reader responsible for following the steps. You're telling them what to do and also engaging their attention:

- You press the green button to open the red door.
- You sound the alarm at volume 5 when the orange light goes on.

How you organize the content is also important. Each step should be either numbered or listed as bullet points in the sequence in which the steps should be followed. This may seem obvious until you have to write directions for complex projects. When this is the case, look at what needs to be done from start to finish, then organize the task into segments, with each segment getting its own set of steps.

When you have written out the directions, ask a colleague to read them with a view to finding any points of confusion or repetition. Revise as needed and then try following them yourself. This can reveal further areas of confusion. Revise again.

The more important it is to get the directions right, the more they should be tested by independent people who will tell you what does and doesn't work.

MAKE TEMPLATES TO USE AND REUSE

Some companies provide a set of templates to make written communication easier. This takes the form of a standard document produced in the company style that you can customize to meet the needs of each situation. If you don't have a set of house-style templates, there are websites offering forms and standardized documents for memos, emails and reports – some free and others at a small cost.

But it's much better to make your own templates because these will suit your own writing style and directly relate to your work issues. Although it takes an investment of time to get started, you save time in future whenever you reuse a previously produced document. You can start by looking at your last month's written material, including emails. Include here business reports you've co-authored if these were written with colleagues from the same business.

Next, categorize these documents and choose the best ones from each category. Define 'best' in terms of their being brief, clear and covering all necessary points. Then cut and paste paragraphs, sentences and phrases from documents in each category. This is a particularly useful activity if there are reports that need to be produced regularly. Remove specific references, but keep the formatting, introductory and concluding sections. Reproduce as needed.

Putting it all together

Anyone can write for business or professional purposes with practice. It is, after all, just putting words together so that they make sense to a reader. However, it also takes a willingness to ask for advice and actively seek criticism from the people who have to read what you write. Their comments won't be personal and you'll gain respect when you ask your colleagues to tell you when they don't understand so that you can improve how and what you write.

The purpose of business and professional writing is to record events in a non-emotional way. This is factual reporting. Rudyard Kipling used a set of questions to organize information and put them into a poem:

> 'I have six honest serving men
> They taught me all I knew
> I call them What and Where and When
> And How and Why and Who.'

Answering these questions can help you focus on what's most important and give structure to your writing.

28 PLAY FOR THE TEAM

'The way a team plays as a whole determines its success. You may have the greatest bunch of individual stars in the world, but if they don't play together, the club won't be worth a dime.'
Babe Ruth

'Alone we can do so little, together we can do so much.'
Helen Keller

'Teamwork is the ability to work together toward a common vision. The ability to direct individual accomplishment toward organizational objectives. It is the fuel that allows common people to attain uncommon results.'
Andrew Carnegie

'No matter how brilliant your mind or strategy, if you're playing a solo game, you'll always lose out to a team.'
Reid Hoffman

'I am constantly being asked about individuals. The only way to win is as a team. Football is not about one or two or three star players.'
Pelé (Edson Arantes do Nascimento)

Can a team really achieve more than the same number of individuals working separately? Henry Ford, founder of the Ford Motor Company, answered this question in 1913 with the installation of the first assembly line. His idea reduced the time to build a car from 12 hours to two-and-a-half by organizing the workforce into separate sections, each of which would contribute a step in the overall process of making the car.

His assembly line idea is teamwork on a grand scale, with mechanized processes bringing parts and completed components from team section to team section within the factory team as a whole. While one team pieces together engines, another fits chassis bodies together, while a third team works on the undercarriage. No single section is more important than another – everyone has offered something crucial to the completed cars.

In recent years, the benefit of working in teams has been referred to as synergy. This is the idea that the whole is greater than the sum of its parts, or 2 + 2 = 5. When two people work with two others, they produce the work of five, not four people. This is true of assembly lines as well as sports teams on the field. Synergy can occur naturally but, to be sure of good results, effort has to be made to produce it.

This is the team leader's job. With the role comes the responsibility to bring people together to create a single effective performance from the contributions of many separate individuals. Team leaders provide a focus point. Like conductors of an orchestra, they remind players to bring forward their part, play more loudly or softly, stop suddenly or start slowly. It's best when they offer a light degree of control, but when a team is newly formed they may have to take charge and firmly point the way.

Leading the team by example works best when leaders demonstrate commitment before asking for this from other people. They need to understand what each job requires, even if they've never done it themselves. Not only do teammates appreciate this, but it also helps the team leader estimate how much time and how many resources each team position needs.

BALANCE DOING WORK WITH BUILDING GREAT RELATIONSHIPS

Team leaders have a double assignment: they need to encourage good relationships among all the members while also ensuring that the work gets done. This is called 'balancing task with relationship' and is often presented in graph form, with 'Task' on the x-axis and 'Relationship' on the y-axis.

When a new team forms, more emphasis should be placed on task over relationship because the leader has to explain the work and actively encourage skill building to achieve it. The emphasis on organization over relationship creates a graph with a gently sloping upward line with some focus on relationship but more on task.

In the phase that follows, team members need to get to know one another so that they discover how to play to strengths and manage shared weaknesses. The leader should encourage group discussion and learning so that strong bonds form among team members. The graph line, as a result, rises sharply and peaks.

There's a third phase when team members focus more on task again. Team members still top up on relationship building as new members join the team or problems arise over shared resources, but increasingly they know their jobs and want to get on with them. The graph line peaks and begins to fall.

In the final phase, the team is like a well-oiled machine. Their relationships are now healthy and strong and they can focus on their work. This is also a synergy phase, where team members anticipate needs and respond without being asked. The graph line gently slopes downwards, with emphasis placed on task over relationship.

ADAPT BEHAVIOUR TO SUIT EACH SITUATION

Each of the four development phases described above needs a different leadership style. This means adapting behaviour to meet the changing needs of the team. There are four styles for this: practical, encouraging, delegating and supporting.

- **Practical** – you are friendly but also professional and business-like, as you explain what has to be done. You don't mind a joke and a laugh, but everything is focused on ensuring that the team understands the work it has to do and also the importance of quality, managing resources and deadlines.

- **Encouraging** – the team knows what it has to achieve and has shown initial success. You already know everyone's strengths and weaknesses and now your job is to ensure that everyone on the team knows this as well so that they can anticipate when their fellow team members may need help and support. A 'no blame' culture is created during this phase. You ensure that everyone knows it's safe to make mistakes because colleagues are there to offer support.
- **Delegating** – all the hard work of team building now pays off because you can delegate almost any task to any team member. They know their work and they know one another. There may be friction among members and rivalries – this is normal within any team – but they accept each other and are professional in all their dealings.
- **Supporting** – your style in this phase is almost no style at all. You're more a focus and referral point that guides work to conclusion. The team does the work as you offer support.

CLARIFY TEAM ROLES AND RESPONSIBILITIES

In Secret 4, *Surround yourself with smart people,* Meredith Belbin's team roles model is used to show how to ensure a good mix of abilities on your team. A further step is to clarify roles and responsibilities so that people know what's expected of them. All healthy and well-led teams have these five essentials:

1. **Clear goals** – what the team should achieve in both the long and short term
2. **Rules and processes** – accepted standards of behaviour and how work should be done
3. **Defined roles** – duties and responsibilities assigned to each team member
4. **Relationships** – bonds that hold the team together, mutual trust and commitment
5. **Leadership** – the individual who translates goals into daily priorities, who acts as team champion, and who encourages team members to do their best

Putting it all together

Teamwork makes a difference to productivity, efficiency and motivation. People are happier when working in teams. They know what they are supposed to do because they have team goals and an identified role within the team. Although teams blend skills and abilities, strong individuals are equally important – the stronger the better – as long as they are willing to join forces and co-operate with their teammates.

Every person on a team has to feel that he or she matters and everyone is encouraged to play to the others' strengths. This enables these strong individuals to work well together. It's the team leader's job to know each person's strengths and weaknesses.

As described above, the team leader should recognize the stages in a team's development and adapt behaviour to serve team needs at each stage. Although the first stage says the leader's job is explaining the task, it's also learning all about each team member. Taking an interest in members as people is one way the leader draws the team together. This people-focused style then serves as an example for others on the team to follow.

29 MOTIVATE YOURSELF AND OTHERS

'Our greatest weakness lies in giving up. The most certain way to succeed is always to try just one more time.'
Thomas Alva Edison

'The will to win, the desire to succeed, the urge to reach your full potential... these are the keys that will unlock the door to personal excellence.'
Confucius

'With the new day comes new strength and new thoughts.'
Eleanor Roosevelt

'Do the difficult things while they are easy and do the great things while they are small. A journey of a thousand miles must begin with a single step.'
Lao Tzu

'Do the one thing you think you cannot do. Fail at it. Try again. Do better the second time. The only people who never tumble are those who never mount the high wire. This is your moment. Own it.'
Oprah Winfrey

What motivates people? Is it money, power, love, fame, achievement for its own sake, or maybe a mixture of all of these? Business and military leaders, teachers and psychologists have all been arguing about this for a long time and they still don't have an answer. It often comes down to the available options and current circumstances, so that a person may feel motivated to pursue a goal one day but feel differently the next.

People are complex. This makes discovering the source of motivation very difficult but also very rewarding when any guesses prove correct. And they are guesses because no one can truly know how another person will react on the day. Boredom is yet another issue: once a challenging goal is achieved, motivation to pursue a similar goal will be less intense. This can seem irrational to a leader who wants that next version of a project to receive the same commitment as the first, but people are so often unreasonable. Their motivation fluctuates and also they may not tell the truth about what they want from work. This can be frustrating to their leaders and annoying to their colleagues.

- 'I offered her all the money she wanted, but she left anyway!'
- 'He told me he wanted that project, and now he's barely touched it.'
- 'They committed to arriving on time if we increased their pay, but now they're late every day!'

A leader's job is sometimes not a happy one because people are so often unpredictable. There's a saying, 'You can lead a horse to water but you cannot make it drink.' This has the ring of truth because drinking, unlike being led, is a matter of choice. Anything personal is always choice and leaders need to remember this at all times if they want results.

Motivation comes from within. When the drive, need or expectation is clear within a person, motivation is easier to read and understand. When there's any confusion about values, priorities or essential needs, people will make contradictory demands and even change their minds on a daily basis. It's as if the horse goes to the water's edge, looks at the water and walks away. Then it turns around and makes a beeline to get a drink after all. However, there are a few basics about motivation that can help leaders understand their colleagues better. These can at least provide an agreed starting point for a discussion.

EXPLORE WHAT DRIVES YOU FORWARD

Learning to understand what motivates other people starts by exploring what motivates you. People are motivated by similar things and in many of the same ways, regardless of age, gender, background or culture. This enables you to use your own feelings as a guide to knowing what drives other people. This is still a big challenge, however, because you are just as complicated as everyone else.

Motivation comes from within. It starts as an impulse or an idea to act, and its source can be biological, emotional, intellectual, social or inspirational, among other things. You can be conscious of feeling motivated by a goal or to fulfil a specific need, or you can also be entirely unconscious of what drives you. The motive is there in front of you, but you may not know its origins.

For example, you may believe you work hard as a choice to earn more money, gain status or have a better office. But your underlying motive could easily be something else, like a wish to please your parents. You may realize this only when you feel so much pleasure when you tell them about a promotion or work-related success. Strong drivers can be hidden and even explained away, with more superficial reasons taking their place. As a leader, the better you understand what drives you, the easier it will be to understand your colleagues when they try to explain what they want.

LEARN WHAT THE EXPERTS SAY

Experts say that there are five important motivation theories that explain what drives people to act the way they do, and these are listed below. As you read the list, ask yourself whether you are more comfortable with one theory over another. No single theory tells the whole story. You can learn from each set of ideas to create an effective and motivating leadership style.

- **Carrots and sticks.** This theory uses reward and punishment to drive people to do what you want. But this old-fashioned idea succeeds only when there is very close supervision. People resent you and, as soon as you turn your back, they stop co-operating so that you need to use an even bigger stick.

- **Need to survive and thrive.** People have a drive to meet their needs, whether physical, emotional, intellectual or spiritual. This theory has many variations and is widely used to explain the drive to grow and succeed.
- **Everyone wants to be treated fairly.** Civil service examinations and merit-based hiring are results of this theory, but leaders need to show that fairness standards are followed or all the hard work to be fair can seem unfair after all.
- **Keeping promises is important.** Leaders must avoid making promises they cannot keep because this disappoints and demotivates people when plans sometimes fall though. It's better not to promise anything than to break your word.
- **Goals and a shared direction keep everyone moving.** This theory suggests that goals can be used to encourage motivation. Focusing on the goal encourages commitment and drive to achieve it. This works for motivation, however, only if the goal is beneficial in some way to the person working on it.

IDENTIFY WHAT YOU WANT MOST

Motivation theories help most when you also pay attention to each person's individual preferences and are aware that people want different things. Motivation isn't a question of 'one size fits all'. As a leader, you need to discover what each individual wants and values, and avoid assuming that everyone wants the same thing.

Even twins can want very different things, with one wanting to travel and the other to stay at home. As a result, one will save for a trip and the other will work long hours to buy a house. It's no use helping the one who wants to travel learn more about mortgages or sending the one who wants a house on a modern languages course.

Psychologists say that people want to pursue four kinds of need. You'll encourage their motivation and commitment if you assign work and give rewards that are aligned to what they really want. The four drivers are:

- **power and influence** – wanting to make an impact and be recognized for it

- **friendship** – the need to have harmony in relationships and to help other people
- **achievement** – fairness, independence and concentration are most valued
- **balance** – seeing many different points of view and avoiding extremes.

Putting it all together

Understand yourself and the rest will follow is a good principle when you want to make sense of motivation. Just take a look at your own choices in the last six months, and ask yourself whether they all make sense or if some decisions you made contradict others. Following fleeting social media trends or having to buy the latest fad are as much examples of motivation as wanting to have a pay rise.

Motivation is a drive that can be difficult to explain later. Recognizing this in you may make it easier to accept irrational-seeming behaviour in others. Even erratic behaviour makes sense when you think that personality and activity are influenced by layer on layer of experience. Some past experience and beliefs can create contradictions.

Behaviour you observe may not always seem sensible, but there will be a reason for that person to be driven to do that thing in that way. Learning more about motivation makes you a more effective leader because you see and understand other people with greater clarity. This will help you lead.

30 BE COURTEOUS TO EVERYONE ALWAYS

'Don't flatter yourself that friendship authorizes you to say disagreeable things to your intimates. The nearer you come into relation with a person, the more necessary do tact and courtesy become.'
Oliver Wendell Holmes, Jr.

'When music and courtesy are better understood and appreciated, there will be no war.'
Confucius

'There is something more – the spirit, or the soul. I think that that quality encourages our courtesy and care and our minds. And mercy, and identity.'
Maya Angelou

'Courtesy is the one coin you can never have too much of or be stingy with.'
John Wanamaker

'Gratitude is the most exquisite form of courtesy.'
Jacques Maritain

There are people who never say 'thank you'. They believe that even a hint of gratitude shows weakness and puts them in an inferior position. They think that other people should be grateful to them, not the reverse. This is a lonely way to live, however, because the ungrateful always end up alone. It's gratitude that confirms the bond between giver and receiver and every language has a phrase to mark exchanges, gifts and recognition. Saying 'thanks' acknowledges sharing.

Dame Mary Douglas, the anthropologist, wrote that every culture has a code of behaviour that ensures order and stability and protects against corruption. Only people at the margins of a society disobey these courtesies. In other words, politeness and good manners are ways to ensure a healthy exchange between strangers as well as friends. In contrast to this, a famous self-help guru tells followers never to apologize because this gives other people a hold on them.

By 'hold' he means a feeling of duty or being in debt to another person. But what's wrong with that? What's wrong with people having a hold over one another? Community is based on holds and bonds. Shared ideas lead directly to a mutual commitment to work and be together and this requires people to have a hold on one another. Discourtesy is actually a show of weakness and reveals a fear of other people's strength. By contrast, courtesy is the glue that holds community together.

It's the ritual that enables the strong to live next to the weak in harmony. But new formulas for courtesy can be slow to develop and may not keep pace with social inventions. For example, the use of mobile phones is relatively new on trains, in theatres or during meals. It annoys some people but seems necessary to others, with the phone-using lobby taking an aggressive stance.

It will take time for phone etiquette to emerge. In cultures where expressive talking in public is accepted as normal, phones will continue to ring everywhere and users will escape criticism. But in cultures where loud voices in public are disliked, phone users will gradually modify their behaviour in order to fit in with the majority. People are social animals. If their discourtesy leads to their exclusion from the group, eventually they will change their behaviour.

BE POLITE EVEN WHEN PROVOKED

The phone rings on a busy Saturday morning when you're waiting for a call from a family member. A young voice asks you whether you would like to save money on purchase of prescription drugs, or possibly whether you have considered changing your car insurance – or even if it's time to install new double-glazing. You manage to remain calm throughout, although it takes a big effort, then say 'no thanks' and hang up.

Not only were you courteous, but you did your health a lot of good. Expressing anger with sarcasm, shouting or making rude remarks actually harms your body because it increases your heart rate and blood pressure. You also breathe more quickly and your temperature rises. Even when anger is justified, you still experience adrenaline and cortisol flooding into your bloodstream, and put a strain on your heart. Remaining calm avoids this chemical onslaught, so that a polite 'no thanks' is a very good thing.

This carries over to work situations. Unfair treatment or criticism, rudeness or nastiness often leads to wanting to respond in kind. Mentally counting to ten while choosing to be polite is by far the wiser because healthier choice. Of course, there are times when expressing anger is appropriate and necessary, but it's better if these occasions are rare. Instead, have a policy of being polite, *particularly* when provoked.

MAKE COURTESY A HABIT

There's a saying: 'Be nice to people on the way up because you may see them again on the way down.' Leadership is such a roller-coaster ride that it's surprising everyone doesn't follow this advice. But they don't. There will always be the temptation to use a sharp tone of voice when under pressure, sarcasm when a colleague is pushy, or angry words when your work is criticized unfairly. But it's a mistake to imagine that people will understand and believe that your rudeness is justified.

Anyone watching is more likely to decide they dislike what they see and turn away. People rarely consider that other people's manners are temporary. They see what they see. They also judge rudeness harshly because it's so hard to accept, regardless of the reason. Bad behaviour can also become a habit: pressure then rudeness; pressure then rudeness; then repeat for ever. After a while, the behaviour becomes a permanent style that no one dares challenge.

The way forward is to shine a very bright light on personal behaviour and evaluate whether it's good enough; that is, whether it meets your own standards for others. This should be done regularly because habits form gradually and unconsciously. Newly acquired behaviour is more easily changed. The goal is being a civilized and positive presence at work, at home and in social groups. An ability to be courteous when under pressure is a worthwhile goal.

PRACTISE IMPULSE CONTROL AS A WAY OF LIFE

Who hasn't had the experience of asking, 'Why did I do that?' accompanied by head shaking, sweaty palms and a heartfelt desire to go back in time. There may even be a groan or moan attached. There's also the variation to this: 'Why did you do that?' asked in an accusing tone by someone else.

The issue is easy: impulse control or, rather, the lack of it, when you may have used an inappropriate word or behaviour. This is what it means to be gauche, caught on the wrong foot, bumptious or rude. There are so many words to describe a failure of impulse control. This is because it happens so frequently – absolutely everyone makes a social mistake at one time or another. The antidote is making it a way of life to match behaviour and style to each changing situation.

Brain science explains that there is an area of the brain called the prefrontal cortex that manages choice making. This works with other areas to control and suppress urges and also manage emotion. The good news is that impulse control is learned behaviour. Anyone can develop it with practice. Impulse control is similar to willpower. You get it by saying no to things that are unhelpful and yes to those you believe are good for you.

The more you exercise self-control, the easier it becomes.

Courtesy works. It allows the weak to live with the strong and protects the strong when they inevitably become weak. It also relieves stress. Etiquette is a guide for behaviour and anyone can learn it with minimal effort. It's also the basis for social skill and so it is an essential living skill. If followed, it shows a person how to join a group and then be made welcome there.

Leaders set the tone for the way people behave in the groups they lead. They make everyone's lives so much easier when they reward courtesy and are critical of rudeness. Encouraging mutual respect creates a positive working atmosphere and team spirit. Bullying, gossip and even petty theft cannot gain a toehold in a workplace guided by courtesy.

Clients and customers also appreciate being treated well. It's as if they are seen as people, not just sources of business. Making eye contact, saying 'please', remembering to add 'thank you' following a sale, are all examples of behaviour that costs nothing. But customers will reward you for it. When price, delivery, quality and expertise are equally balanced among competitors, the one that has a history of courtesy will get the business.

31 NEVER GIVE UP

'Never doubt that a small group of committed citizens can change the world. Indeed it is the only thing that ever has.'
Margaret Mead

'It's hard to beat a person who never gives up.'
Babe Ruth

'If you fall behind, run faster. Never give up, never surrender, and rise up against the odds.'
Jesse Jackson

'Most of the important things in the world have been accomplished by people who have kept on trying when there seemed to be no hope at all.'
Dale Carnegie

'If you live long enough, you'll make mistakes. But if you learn from them, you'll be a better person. It's how you handle adversity, not how it affects you. The main thing is never quit, never quit, never quit.'
William J. Clinton

During the Second World War, as Great Britain suffered defeats in North Africa and Europe, Winston Churchill gave a speech in 1941 to Harrow School, where he told the assembled schoolboys:

Never give in. Never give in. Never, never, never, never – in nothing, great or small, large or petty – never give in, except to convictions of honour and good sense. Never yield to force. Never yield to the apparently overwhelming might of the enemy.

This was exactly what they wanted to hear at that time. Leaders like Churchill bring people together during a time of crisis. Their fighting spirit inspires, raises morale and keeps everyone moving steadily forward. But if values shift after the crisis passes, giving up can become a more attractive option than fighting on. People become tired of never giving up and long for an even slightly easier time.

When this occurs, the majority choice is *not* standing firm with its leader. In business, this happens when a company's executive team works hard to convince shareholders to vote no to a rival company's takeover. If the promise of making more money under new management is a powerful enough lure, or there is another compelling reason, then voters will go against their executives. No matter how hard they fight, it won't change the vote if the shareholders want a different result.

Whatever the outcome of the battle – *yes* for Churchill at Harrow and *no* for the business leaders – the results of never giving up always come at great personal cost to leaders. Never giving up means constant pressure to find solutions, even as variations to the original problem pop to the surface. Doubt, fear and self-criticism are ever present. Colleagues, family and friends may even demand an explanation for all the risk-taking as they pressure the leader to stop.

This is why the decision never to give up should always be linked to deeply held beliefs. The desired end result should also be measured against the 'honour and good sense' that Churchill recommends. Then, when the leader's energy falters, as it inevitably will, a sense of purpose and commitment to personal values keeps momentum going. Strongly held beliefs will fuel the drive to succeed and may even keep the leader's self-doubt to a minimum.

AVOID COMPARISONS

There's a classic film in which sprinting racers are coming to the finish line. The camera catches the frontrunner when just a few feet from the tape as he turns his head just a fraction to look back. That glance unfortunately takes a critical second and breaks his concentration just as the nearest contender powers up. The result is second place for him, with the more focused runner in first.

Comparisons are like that. They cost valuable time and create unnecessary distraction from getting the job done. It's also meaningless to compare yourself with others because everyone has a unique style of working and each project has its own cycle. At times, progress can be easy and at others it's painfully slow. Your efforts could be peaking while a competitor's are in a dip, or it could be the reverse.

Not giving up has everything to do with you and nothing to do with anyone or anything else. Determination comes from within and grows every time you tell yourself to keep going against the odds. This sounds self-centred and it is, but in a good way. Awareness of your inner strength, your centre of gravity, is what gets you across the finish line. Your ability to amplify your strengths and manage your weaknesses gets you first place.

SET INTERMEDIATE GOALS

Setting intermediate goals is a useful way to measure progress and is very helpful when managing a long and complex project. Intermediate goals keep you moving towards a major goal and are like signposts positioned at intervals along the way. Achieving each intermediate goal tells you that you are on the right track as well as keeping to time.

Although you keep your eyes on the prize of the major goal, you also push to reach each signpost knowing that, if you do this, success will eventually be yours. The number and spacing of intermediate goals depend upon your major goal – its estimated time to completion and stages of development – as well as on alliances and co-operating individuals or groups.

Alternatively, they can be linked to anticipated peaks and troughs as a way to pace activity overall. For example, if you think it likely that motivation will dip after a major effort, then identify at least one feature of the effort that you are 100-per-cent certain can be achieved. This will give you an excuse to say 'Congratulations!' on achieving this intermediate goal.

For example, when energy starts to dip, schedule a meeting to review recent performance. Feature all the successes that led to that stage of the project. Also, analyse any failures such as missed deadlines or failed communication. Celebrate both the successes and anything learned from mistakes. This will give everyone the burst of energy they need to move through a dip in spirits.

MAINTAIN GOOD SPIRITS

When the pressure is on and everyone around you is ready to give up, your steady and continued optimism can make all the difference. Leaders are the only ones who must believe in a happy ending. Everyone else can falter, but not you. Maintaining good spirits is a way to inspire not only your own motivation but also renewed motivation in your colleagues. A positive attitude brings you closer to achieving your goals.

There's a well-known technique recommended by psychologists that can help you project positive feelings and confidence, even if you dread the times ahead. It's called 'Acting as if' and, just as the name describes, it means that you behave as if you *are* actually what you *should be* in that situation. Your acting as if you have more confidence means you use big gestures, a strong tone of voice and facial expressions that show you are very confident indeed.

Surprisingly, this works and it is backed by several research studies. For example, you may want to show your authority to ensure that deadlines are met, but you feel tired, anxious and almost certain that the project will fail. Instead of giving in to these feelings, you put on your 'game face' and show a strong, disciplined and confident manner. Your colleagues immediately pick up on this and copy you.

'Acting as if' may begin as a performance but very soon becomes genuine self-expression.

Putting it all together

The word 'never' sounds extreme. How can anyone plan on never doing, saying or being something? For this reason, some leaders never make that promise. But never giving up is an attitude rather than a promise. When Winston Churchill told the Harrow schoolboys never to give in, he meant that they needed a fighting spirit and the will to keep going until every bit of strength, resource and energy they had was gone. His message is that leaders keep going and maintain their courage as an essential part of their job.

This could seem like dramatizing leadership and, for less urgent or minor projects, it's not necessary to think about never giving up. Maintaining a fighting spirit in everyday life is an uncomfortable idea. But if your values and beliefs do require you to give a project your full support, then – even if it's a dramatic gesture – you will need to decide where you draw your line and when you say, 'I will not give up on this.'

Delivering this promise can be made easier if you organize it into smaller sections, and then work out how to reach each section's end, in what time, and with what means. Fighting your way forward, step by step in this way, is far less daunting and also more doable.

32 COUNT THE COST OF SOLVING PROBLEMS

'The fishermen know that the sea is dangerous and the storm terrible, but they have never found these dangers sufficient reason for remaining ashore.'
Vincent van Gogh

'There are only two mistakes one can make along the road to truth; not going all the way, and not starting.'
Siddhārtha Gautama Buddha

'If you're going through hell, keep going.'
Winston Churchill

'Do not think of today's failures, but of the success that may come tomorrow.'
Helen Keller

'Give me six hours to chop down a tree and I will spend the first four sharpening the axe.'
Abraham Lincoln

There are inspiring stories of inventors, explorers and athletes who put everything into solving an important problem or achieving an impossible goal. Their commitment and dedication are an inspiration. For example, Florence Nightingale not only launched professional nursing but also lobbied for change in public health and pioneered the use of practical statistics to illustrate patient mortality. Her life was devoted to public service, although in the process she ruined her own health.

She would have argued that it was worth it. But not all goals are equal. Problem solvers and business leaders in everyday life study spreadsheets, decide budgets and manage resources for commercial reasons. This is important, even crucial, for the business but will not necessarily change the world for the better or be worth a leader's 100-per-cent dedication to the exclusion of everything else.

So how does a leader decide which project receives unlimited resources and which gets more measured support? It's an important issue because when full attention is given to one challenge, other projects will receive much less. Leaders need to know when enough is enough and, alternatively, when to throw every resource into achieving the goal.

The issue is priority. As an example, in 1962 President John Kennedy announced that the United States would land a man on the moon within the next decade. It would cost a phenomenal amount and would require national commitment to make it happen, but US politicians at that time believed it was a crucial choice. Their then Cold War enemy, the Soviet Union, had launched a satellite and this was considered a threat to national security.

The right or wrong of this is another issue. The point is that people will ignore cost when they are under threat, in competition or driven by a dream. But the reckoning will always arrive and leaders will have to account for their choices. Sometimes it's only after the cost is finally counted that it becomes clear whether the resources were wisely used or wasted. This secret is about deciding sooner rather than later when it's smarter to stop or carry on regardless.

IDENTIFY REALISTIC COSTS

There are three costs that need reckoning before any big commitment is made. They are materials, morale and money – in that order. Materials are the resources a project needs for its completion. If you don't have what is needed, you must acquire it or, if necessary, invent it. For example, when Florence Nightingale wanted to make her case for an improved sanitation system, she lacked a model or methodology to show statistics visually. The result was her invention of the pie chart and her pioneering of graphical methods to illustrate her numerical evidence.

Morale in a working group is also extremely important, and this includes your own morale. If a project needs support and the people involved are uncommitted, you will need to find a different set of people or a way to work alone. Poor morale and lack of commitment undermine a project. Your colleagues must be 100 per cent with you and as leader your job is to encourage this. A half-hearted effort from disenchanted people is bound to fail.

Money is the great divider, truth-teller and project killer, and it is another key ingredient of success. However, it's also potentially more accessible than either materials or morale. After calculating what you need, including funds for emergencies and the unexpected, you'll know clearly whether you have the funds available. If not, then you can fundraise, look for backers or seek loans. This is difficult, but it's the easiest of the three costs to acquire.

KNOW WHAT YOU WANT TO ACHIEVE

This strategy refers to the spirit driving your goal. For example, this could be launching a new product line. Before identifying costs, ask yourself what benefit you hope to gain from this. Do you want to add a new revenue stream, increase your customer base, enhance your brand, or something else? Your answer tells you what likely costs will arise. You can then identify cost-effective ways to serve your goal.

For example, if the benefit you want is an increase in revenue, you could revise your goal so that it emphasizes this. Instead of launching a new line, you would update an existing line in a way that encourages re-buy by existing customers. This could also attract new customers if the marketing programme emphasizes the new updates. The result would be increased revenue without risk of launching a new product or additional R&D costs.

Redefining your goal like this goes to the source of the problem. Look at the following list of questions. Answer them to gain a better understanding of both your problem and how you can achieve a lasting solution.

- What problem needs a solution?
- What features of the problem need greater clarity?
- What additional information will help redefine the problem?
- What goal or solution can solve this problem?

UNDERSTAND YOUR OWN FEAR OF LOSS

When deciding whether to continue with a project that's costing more money than planned, you need to factor in your own fear of losing. This can have a powerful impact on your decision to go ahead or put a stop to a project. Psychologists say that, when you set goals and think in terms of all the gains you'll receive, you tend to tolerate mistakes and losses more easily in pursuit of your goal. They call this having a promotion focus.

Alternatively, you have a prevention focus when you think about how much you'll lose if you don't achieve the goal. Ironically, a prevention focus tends to hinder your ability to cut your losses, while a promotion focus supports your ability to analyse a situation and then say 'no thanks' in a timely manner. This is because when you focus on gaining, you are more likely to see a disastrous situation for what it is. Your analysis will produce a 'yikes' moment as you reflect, 'There's nothing to gain from this. I want out.'

No one likes to lose. So when deciding to cut your losses, if you focus on what you're likely to lose in terms of energy, time or financial investment, you are more likely to keep going. Fear of losing can grip you, and then emotions can cloud your judgement. Every project needs built-in evaluation stages at regular intervals that force you to reflect on what you have to gain by cutting your losses at that stage.

Putting it all together

It's so often the case that when a business, project or activity fails it's because the problems weren't solved on time and at first. Problem solving is a core part of every leader's job and the degree of skill he or she brings to this either creates growth or causes stagnation. Skill has to be driven by disciplined and creative thinking.

Thinking about the problem in a new way helps. To do this, go to the problem's source to revisit what caused things to go wrong in the first place. This can reveal new information. You may then:

- find alternative ways to think about the problem
- identify different desired benefits from solving the problem
- discover a different problem that is more urgent to solve.

Problem solving is also a psychological issue. Leaders' fears for the future and their ambition can cloud judgement so that they forget the reason the problem needs to be solved. They can become sidetracked into settling a personal score. This is the source of empire building, with a blindly determined CEO gambling everything on an expansion that makes no sense in terms of real growth for the business.

33 ENCOURAGE OTHERS TO DEVELOP AND GROW

'As we look ahead into the next century, leaders will be those who empower others.'

Bill Gates

'If your actions inspire others to dream more, learn more, do more and become more, you are a leader.'

John Quincy Adams

'Leaders must wake people out of inertia. They must get people excited about something they've never seen before, something that does not yet exist.'

Rosabeth Moss Kanter

'The day soldiers stop bringing you their problems is the day you have stopped leading them.'

Colin Powell

'Our chief want is someone who will inspire us to be what we know we could be.'

Ralph Waldo Emerson

Many psychologists agree that people have a drive to grow and live healthy lives. Even when circumstances stop their development so that their talent is ignored, their skills are unperfected and their ambition is unfulfilled, with encouragement people can still shake off the past and accept new challenges – just because they can. This is why trekkers climb mountains, athletes stretch their limits, and very smart people accept low-paid jobs in public service areas such as teaching and policing. They want to do and be more.

Secret 4, *Surround yourself with smart people*, describes the benefits of working with strong, creative and challenging people. Sometimes these colleagues are already in post or are recruited fully developed, but most often they grow into bigger jobs as a result of opportunities given to them through their current work. Leadership supports people growing in this way by creating an atmosphere that welcomes and encourages development.

Those leaders who see potential in their colleagues and encourage them to express themselves do both their organizations and themselves a favour. Not only are they enabling talent to do a better job, they are also inspiring loyalty. People who feel valued and supported return these feelings with gratitude. Later, if they are asked to work harder and do more with less, they just do it. When asked why, many explain that they feel connected to the team and loyal to their boss.

Connection creates a sense of community and begins a virtuous circle of colleagues being encouraged to fulfil their potential so that, in turn, they want to support those who encouraged them in the first place. This sparks further connection and the circle of encouragement and mutual support begins again. There is extensive research showing that employees who feel connected to their work and value their colleagues are more productive and generate more profit.

The introduction to this book refers to employee empowerment. This begins with a leader listening to the workforce, hearing employee ideas, and bringing benefit to the business as a result. Rather than forcing an efficiency drive from the top, empowered employees identify improved procedures and implement these themselves. Those organizations that have yet to discover the merits of empowerment need a wake-up call. Modern business needs a motivated workforce and leaders who encourage this.

BE AN EXAMPLE OF HEALTHY GROWTH

If you are committed to personal development yourself – that is, you take courses, exhibit an inquiring mind, seek to understand other people's points of view, engage in debate, and learn and grow as a result – then those around you will be likely to want to join you in being positive. By contrast, if you are fixed to your desk, exhibit no ambition, take the line of least resistance and avoid any extra thinking whatsoever, it is equally likely that your best employees will transfer away as fast as the paperwork can be processed.

As a leader you can never stagnate because your job is to show the way forward, to identify and then integrate new ideas, and to have your finger on the world pulse as trends emerge and forces drive events. This is possible because communication is so fast. It also makes you far more visible. Think of someone who is unaware of the need for skill in digital technology. Is this someone you find inspiring?

Performance review requires asking your colleagues about their career plans and development needs. If you've already set an example of personal growth, then expecting your colleagues to want to grow as well has credibility. Encouraging other people to develop their potential also further pressures you to discover new ways to clarify your own future plans. This is your chance to rediscover hobbies and interests you've left undeveloped.

ENCOURAGE AMBITION AND ASK FOR STRETCH

Using the **path–goal model** is a good way to encourage yourself and others to stretch existing skills and develop new ones. It requires you, as a leader, to make it easy for employees to achieve their assigned goals. This works by first explaining what the goals are, and then deciding how these can be achieved. You should do this together, asking for ideas and making suggestions until the path to reach the goal is clearly defined.

This leadership style requires you to be both supportive and demanding in turn, based on the employee's maturity or level of expertise. You can choose from four approaches:

- **Supportive** – focus on the individual's personal development
- **Directive** – guide complex work when the person is inexperienced

- **Consultative** – draw on the person's expertise to co-plan how to do the work
- **Achieving** – encourage new ideas; give the person a chance to excel

After determining the path, your job as leader is to clear any obstacles to reaching the goals. At first, this approach may seem harder than telling people what to do and watching them carefully to ensure that it's done. However, you get more work done to a higher standard with this approach and employees will feel more highly motivated. Your own work will also become more interesting as you play educator, psychologist and adviser in sequence. Path–goal supports the individual as well as the organization.

USE PREVIEW–REVIEW TO CREATE CONTINUOUS IMPROVEMENT

Preview–review is a technique that helps you evaluate past experience in order to improve future performance. It supports learning through trial and error because you focus exclusively on the most recent trial, analyse exactly what happened in a detailed review, and then produce a checklist of suggestions for improving your next performance.

This checklist prepares you for the next trial. It allows you to set realistic improvement goals because these are based directly on actual performance. The result is steady and organic, continuous improvement, using critique from self and others and evaluation of the circumstances surrounding each event. This systematic review describes what actually happened, with strengths and weaknesses highlighted.

With sports it can mean cutting as much as a second from an athlete's best time; with business it can mean an additional percentage point of profit on a sale. In a review you are looking for specific examples of weaknesses such as errors of judgement, hesitation, emotional resistance, fear, poor or confused support, or wrong timing, lack of or inadequate facilities, and much more. You also want to identify areas of strength to build upon those.

Furthermore

When you've used this technique yourself, you can teach it to colleagues. Although a generic checklist would help, there are too many variables to produce a list that has credibility. Instead, consider these areas: timing, place, people, transportation, facilities and materials, and produce your own checklist.

Putting it all together

One of a leader's most important jobs is encouraging colleagues to grow. This creates a significant saving in the recruitment budget because key staff develop organically from within the business rather than being hired from outside. Some leaders protest that investing in people risks wasting money because they could leave after training. This may be true when work is always routine and there is little hope of career advancement. However, you will create an atmosphere of efficiency and growth as everyone gains skill. As new people replace the ambitious ones who leave, they join a workforce that has higher quality and production standards. Trained people raise the performance of the people around them. This makes everyone look good, including you.

People never forget the person who made a difference in their lives and encouraged them to believe they could do and be more. This could be as simple as finding something positive to comment about in their work, saying 'Well done!' when a deadline is met, or encouraging them to take a course so that they can gain skills to improve their career. This makes the leader an educator and adds to job satisfaction.

34 BE APPROACHABLE

'This is important: to get to know people, listen, expand the circle of ideas. The world is crisscrossed by roads that come closer together and move apart, but the important thing is that they lead towards the Good.'
Pope Francis

'The best weapon of a dictatorship is secrecy, but the best weapon of a democracy should be the weapon of openness.'
Niels Bohr

'We shall never know all the good that a simple smile can do.'
Mother Teresa

'I often compare open source to science. To where science took this whole notion of developing ideas in the open and improving on other people's ideas and making it into what science is today and the incredible advances that we have had. And I compare that to witchcraft and alchemy, where openness was something you didn't do.'
Linus Torvalds

'You either believe that people respond to authority, or that they respond to kindness and inclusion. I'm obviously in the latter camp. I think that people respond better to reward than punishment.'
Brian Eno

Stanley Gertz likes to arrive early to his office. He has a small coffee maker – a gift from his wife – that his secretary sets up for him at the end of every working day. All Stanley has to do in the morning is press the button and the machine grinds fresh beans and then brews his coffee while he checks his emails.

After about an hour, Stanley hears his workforce of about
15 people get to their desks. His door is closed but he can
watch them from the webcams he installed himself one Sunday
afternoon years before. He likes the feeling of seeing but not
being seen and he's sure that no one knows about the cams.
He then works steadily until 10:30, when he opens his door
and walks around the office, saying good morning and smiling
at each member of staff individually. Stanley has been on a
leadership course and learned that this is something people want,
although he doesn't really understand why. If he never saw his
own boss again, it would still be too soon.

Just thinking of the weekly managers' meeting makes him frown.
But that ordeal is set in stone, and so of course he goes. Stanley
has to work, although he's just past retirement age. There are still
very big bills from his wife's cancer treatment and if he can stay
in work for another two years, they will be out of debt. So he
grins – well, not quite – and bears it.

Marie Lamb looks up from her desk as Stanley approaches. He's
such a good person and she wishes that he knew that everyone
laughs at him – even his own boss. Every day he has the same
routine. He always remembers to ask about her mother, who has
recently been seriously ill. Marie doesn't drive and so Stanley
took them to the hospital every single week.

Marie takes the meeting's minutes for the executive committee
and so she knows that Stanley is about to be let go. He has more
than 30 years of service, but they plan to dump him suddenly
without any warning. They call it shock tactics. Marie would
like to warn him to contact an employment lawyer, but he's
so unapproachable that she wouldn't know how to begin the
conversation.

KNOW WHY YOU WANT TO BE APPROACHABLE

Stanley Gertz believes that he should smile and say hello to his
colleagues at work, but he doesn't know why. His translation of
the advice from a leadership course is to walk around the office

mid-morning and greet everyone. This isn't really such an odd thing to do. There are business advice books that advise this behaviour. But Stanley's way of doing it feels false – to him and to the others – and so it doesn't really work.

If he understood why he should smile or say hello, it would make his behaviour seem more natural and as a result make him more approachable. This change would benefit him as well as his colleagues, giving him, a shy person, the chance to connect properly with people in an informal but professional way. Connection is a necessity in every workplace because it speeds exchange of information, gets questions answered, shares the workload, and much more. It's what creates the system of people interacting with one another, directly and indirectly. Organizations of every size are really run by these internal networks. They form a community that provides mutual support to all its members.

Here are a few questions to help you decide whether you are an approachable member of your workplace community. In the last week:

- has anyone at work offered you a suggestion without being invited?
- have you asked any colleagues for their ideas?
- has everyone you've approached reacted as if your approach is normal?

You should have answered yes to each question. If you didn't, do you know why? For example, a young intern or a newly hired person might have felt surprised because they don't know you.

ASK QUESTIONS AND LISTEN TO THE ANSWERS

When Stanley asks Marie about her mother, he's sincerely interested. He's proved this by driving them to hospital weekly. But others in his office don't know about this side of his personality. They ridicule what seems to be his play-acting at being friendly. And, in fairness to them, his behaviour must seem unnatural, because for him it is.

Approachable leaders have to *want* to be interested in how others are doing. It's their job to know when support is needed or whether questions and problems have arisen. The way they find out is by asking and then listening to the answers. Sincerity can and should be telegraphed with tone of voice and a friendly manner because this shows genuine interest more than the content of any questions asked.

An abrupt 'You all right?' among people who know one another well can be a warm greeting if that's their normal speaking style. Leaders or anyone newly joining a work group need to learn what's normal and what being approachable means to that group. Stanley never learned what his colleagues think is normal. He watches them secretly through a webcam, but doesn't hear how they speak to one another. The result is that he doesn't know how to fit in and be approachable.

SHARE NEWS ABOUT YOURSELF

Reactions to being left out of the loop can include hurt feelings, indifference, anger, annoyance, frustration or amusement. However, the crucial reaction should be concern at the possibility of being an unapproachable person. Lack of inclusion in news, plans and general opinions means that there isn't a finger on work life's pulse. Everyone needs this to some degree, but leaders must have it always.

It's how you learn that an important colleague is unhappy enough to leave. If you are an approachable person, he or she tells you informally, maybe over coffee, and explains what's going wrong or is frustrating. You in turn listen quietly without urging one action over another. You may have several conversations. If the colleague's concerns are serious, you can start addressing them based on the talks you're having. If they are temporary, just talking through the frustrations may help resolve them.

One way in which you can show you're approachable is by sharing information about yourself. Every leader should have a hobby to talk about at work. It breaks the ice and is just personal enough to show what kind of person you are. For example, if Stanley Gertz kept tropical fish, he could talk about this. Eventually, his kind personality would be revealed through stories about his fish.

Furthermore

Work takes as much as a third of every day and colleagues want to know at least something about the people they sit beside. Hobbies make good starting points for conversation, as do sports, trivia contests or Scrabble competitions. Whether you are very good, very bad or even in the very middle of success at this kind of activity, talking about it makes you a part of things and very much in the loop.

Putting it all together

Part of every leader's job is to be approachable. Even with social media taking a central role in communication at work, it's still vitally important to connect face to face with colleagues in an informal and even casual way. This feeds and supports digital contact, and humanizes and reinforces a sense of connection.

People need to know what's going on around them if they want to be effective and make a positive contribution. Their personal success depends on communication skills and working well with their colleagues. Increasingly, every organization is run as a network of activity. Being approachable is a necessary quality for this.

It takes effort to be approachable, even if you are lucky enough to have a naturally friendly personality. Consistency is crucial so that your friendliness is also your normal professional manner, with everyone receiving a similar reaction and treatment. This is what reassures your colleagues that you'll respond well to their approach.

35 EXAMINE YOUR OWN BEHAVIOUR

'I think self-awareness is probably the most important thing towards being a champion.'
Billie Jean King

'You are what you think. So just think big, believe big, act big, work big, give big, forgive big, laugh big, love big and live big.'
Andrew Carnegie

'Respect your efforts, respect yourself. Self-respect leads to self-discipline. When you have both firmly under your belt, that's real power.'
Clint Eastwood

'When you are content to be simply yourself and don't compare or compete, everybody will respect you.'
Lao Tzu

'When we are no longer able to change a situation, we are challenged to change ourselves.'
Viktor Frankl

Self-examination helps people see their own strengths and weaknesses so that they can develop and grow. In the process, they also increase their self-knowledge. This will always help leaders, who need to draw on their inner resources to make decisions, solve problems, encourage their colleagues, and a lot more besides. It's a reflective skill, however, and so may not feel entirely natural to everyone.

Practical people, or those who just want to get the job done, may think that studying their own motives and behaviour is self-indulgent. The purpose for doing this, however, is to improve their performance as leaders and their behaviour as people.

Decisions made by self-aware leaders are more likely to be connected to their personal values. This strengthens their resolve and commitment to carry forward those decisions.

Self-awareness means having a clear head about what's important so that no matter where their parachute takes them, these leaders have an internal starting point to assess what needs to be done. They know immediately whether they have the necessary capability and, if not, they can still get started if they are the only one available to lead. Knowing their limitations gives them a way to monitor their own performance when no one else is there to offer advice and feedback.

A 2013 study from Stanford University reported that almost all 200 of the CEOs, board members and senior executives taking part in the research project wanted executive coaching with the purpose of developing their self-knowledge. They felt that the harder they worked the more they believed it necessary to discover what else they needed to learn. For these leaders, having self-awareness was very important.

There's a technique called **reflection-on-action** that is used by many health service professionals to help them focus on self-improvement. Because thinking power underlies their ability to assess each situation, they need to keep their minds sharp. Reflection-on-action allows review of professional activities with the intention of learning from experience.

One of the best ways to practise this technique is by keeping a journal. Another is to form a partnership with another like-minded professional for mutual feedback and discussion of performance highs and lows. A third way is to find a coach or mentor to guide improvement in a structured way.

KEEP A REFLECT-ON-ACTION JOURNAL

Warren Buffet, the famously successful investor and one of the five richest people in the world, said in an interview that he always writes down the reasons for investments he makes. Later, he reviews what he wrote to see whether he was right about them. Many others offer the same advice. A journal allows you to express your private thoughts and reactions without censorship or judgement. It can take any form you wish: typed notes on the screen, a bound notebook or an inexpensive scribble pad from the newsagent. The pages can be lined or blank, with the blank ones inviting sketches or even flow charts for your future plans.

Here are a few questions you can use to get started:

- What did I learn today?
- Did I use all the resources I have available?
- What held me back?
- What pushed me forward?
- When did I work well and when not so well?
- What was frustrating?
- What made me happy?
- Did I make any promises?
- Do I have any regrets?

You can decide to use the same questions every day or give yourself a different set or structure. It's best to focus on your motives, intentions, actions and interactions as a way to review and evaluate your professional performance. This kind of journal is for self-assessment rather than recording the events of your day.

PREDICT YOUR FUTURE

Another reflective technique asks you to write down every important decision you make, along with what you expect to happen by the end of the year as result of that decision. This requires thinking about the results of your decision-making in a detailed way, and in advance. A yearly time frame is useful because you can imagine a variety of outcomes within that span.

Decisions tend to be more practical when they are made with the hope of producing needed results. This technique also asks you to explore what kind of events could affect your decision during the year. By looking at the year ahead at intervals of three and six months, you can anticipate what can go wrong and so be prepared for any unintended consequences.

Here are ten steps to predict your future and then evaluate your predictions:

1. What goal should my decision achieve?
2. What drives the decision and what is its purpose?
3. List the actions you plan for the next three months to implement this decision.
4. By the end of three months, what do you expect will result from those actions?
5. If there is more than one result, write about these as well.
6. List any further actions required between months three and six, as based on the results you imagined. Do this for each of the different imagined results in item 5.
7. What do you think will happen as a result of those actions?
8. What do you think the final outcome of the decision will look like in one year?
9. Keep these notes and refer to them in one year.
10. Analyse your actions at the three- and six-month intervals and decide what you did well and what not so well. Improve on this the next time you use this technique.

KNOW WHERE YOU ARE ON THE FOOD CHAIN

The food chain idea was introduced by Al-Jahiz, an African-Arab natural philosopher in the ninth century, and it describes the highly complex way in which organisms interact. A simplified version shows how animals relate in terms of which one eats another. This often appears as a vertical line with animals of increasing fierceness rising one above the other. In one example, sea urchins are on the bottom, with fish above, then seals, then polar bears. Other illustrations show a human as the master predator at the top of the line.

The food chain can be a metaphor for the way people relate to one another in organizational life, with the least powerful person on the bottom and the most predatory at the top. It's always wise to know your place on the food chain because this helps you to identify your own predators. Then you can avoid making them angry, or even avoid meeting them entirely if possible. As an exercise, think of the people you know at work and decide where to place them on a food chain. It's interesting that some people may be higher on a workplace chain but lower on one showing a sporting group chain. The point of this is to match your behaviour to your position. If you want a better position, you can always try to move up.

Putting it all together

Reflection is a skill that you can acquire with practice. It comes naturally to some but is a major challenge for others. However, it supports good leadership and should become part of every leader's toolkit for improving performance. But there has to be a balance. Too much introspection is self-indulgent while too little leads to superficial reactions and attitudes.

Self-knowledge not only enriches life but also increases your effectiveness. With it, decisions are long lasting and better considered, problems also tend to be solved for good, and good relationships develop and run smoothly. All of this is a result of thinking things through before taking action, which avoids unnecessary trouble. Stopping to reflect costs nothing. Ten minutes in the morning to think about what lies ahead and ten minutes at night to reflect on what actually happened are all you need.

36 ENCOURAGE DEBATE

'I'm not shy about heated debate or passionate discourse, but when people get crazy or rude, that's a buzz kill. There's got to be a better code of conduct, some basic etiquette.'
Mos Def (Yasiin Bey)

'For good ideas and true innovation, you need human interaction, conflict, argument, debate.'
Margaret Heffernan

'Historically, the claim of consensus has been the first refuge of scoundrels; it is a way to avoid debate by claiming that the matter is already settled.'
Michael Crichton

'A good leader can engage in a debate frankly and thoroughly, knowing that at the end he and the other side must be closer, and thus emerge stronger. You don't have that idea when you are arrogant, superficial and uninformed.'
Nelson Mandela

'What we have to do is find a way to celebrate our diversity and debate our differences without fracturing our communities.'
Hillary Clinton

One dictionary definition of debate is that it is 'a formal discussion on a particular matter in a public meeting or legislative assembly, in which opposing arguments are put forward and which usually ends with a vote'. Debate occurs in a variety of situations, from the formal parliamentary procedure which is part of British Common Law to adaptations used in every English-speaking country.

Debate is also practised worldwide, with each culture or legal system producing its own set of rules and procedures. For example, French political debate goes on for hours, and its moderators keep their interventions to a minimum. However, there are strict rules that French debaters follow as a point of pride. This allows expression of very strong opinions but also avoids a fight. Debating ritual slows reactions so that warring parties get the chance to have their say while the other side has to listen.

Informal debate takes place everywhere: during committees, in shops, among friends, at meetings and on city streets. One person speaks and then another gives a different view, and third may disagree with both. It's civilized – even if intense – and calm, as long as everyone listens and allows others to speak as well. A danger for informal debate is an angry reaction to different opinions and beliefs.

Disagreeing with a neutral idea is fine, but debating closely held beliefs often creates a flammable situation. When anger takes over, even a discussion about football scores can turn into a furious row. Blood rushes to the brain and reaction times speed up. This is when the shouting starts and the listening stops. Sometimes a peacemaker emerges naturally in a group: someone who slows the argument down with a joke or cheerfully encourages everyone to remain friendly before a full-scale argument breaks out.

Being open about conflicting points of view is healthy and the only real way to resolve differences. But this doesn't happen naturally. People like the sound of their own voices more than that of other people's, and they also like to express their opinions without restriction. In a work situation, it's the leader's job to ensure that everyone listens to differing opinions.

Conflict at work needs a moderator to keep the peace.

IDENTIFY WHEN TO DEBATE

Whenever people gather, there's a potential for conflict. This is most likely when resources are scarce or space is limited. People want to have their fair share, and they will fight to get it or will at least be prepared to do so. This is also true with intangibles like power or status. Conflict can start if someone is perceived to be unfairly favoured over their colleagues – perhaps with a promotion, praise from the boss or even a new lamp for their desk. Different beliefs can also lead to everyone fighting like rats tied up in a bag.

Some people will fight without any cause at all. It could be an adrenaline surge or even a genetic issue that makes them need to argue or prove they are number one and the person in charge. When this urge is channelled, you find these would-be combatants in legal offices all over the world, where they've learned to focus their love of argument by debating the law. These disciplined thinkers are often able debaters. Even when they have strong opinions, they remain calm so that their emotions don't affect their thinking. Instead, it helps them focus, so that they are sharper and more skilled at finding weak points in their opponents' argument. Their mental discipline also helps them debate successfully when they lack commitment to a cause. Their personal views are secondary to their drive to win. Recognizing the potential for conflict helps turn a potential fight into a debate.

WORK WITH THESIS, ANTITHESIS AND SYNTHESIS

If you look again at the definition of a debate above, it describes a presentation of opposing arguments that ends in a vote. This is another way of saying thesis, antithesis and synthesis. The thesis is the starting idea, followed by antithesis, or the opposing idea. Debaters present their arguments in turn, with a purpose of convincing an independent audience that they are right and the other side is wrong. The final vote is the debate's synthesis, or the resolution, of the debaters' conflict.

The art and science of debate developed in ancient Greece as a form of competitive entertainment in the style of 'Greece has talent'. Debaters stood before their fellow citizens to show how clever and sharp-witted they were with debate, as proof of their verbal skill. Less experienced debaters studied the best performers. Eventually, they felt able to step forward and test their skill against them in debating contests. Winning a debate could make them stars.

Leading politicians emerged from these debating displays. Public debate also gave rise to legal representation in the ancient equivalent of a court of law. The unskilled would hire the best debaters to argue their cases. Different debating styles emerged as well as a code of practice for debaters. However, the principles of thesis, antithesis and synthesis remain at the heart of all debate. As a debater, if you stay within these, you'll achieve success.

PREPARE FOR FALL-OUT

When debate goes well and conflict seems resolved by vote, judgement or other means, opposing sides have an opportunity to start again with better understanding. But even the best-made plans can go awry and conflict can break out again. It happens because people can be insincere, badly intentioned, resentful of the outcome or convinced that it's unfair. Encouraging debate is wise, but it won't heal all wounds. In fact, it can open new ones.

This strategy is about preparing for disappointment when debate fails to produce results or when the results it produces turn into a phoney peace. However, debate is still the wise choice even when you know there's a risk of failure. What is your option really: conflict, uncontrolled behaviour, the strong behaving badly toward the weak? With debate and structured discussion, you at least have a very good chance of creating understanding.

There's a sequence that failed agreements follow: debate, vote, agreement, and then renewed conflict. If, or when, this happens, patience is the key. Just begin the cycle again. As soon as hostility re-emerges, in a steady and calm manner renew the discussion and debate. However long it takes, it is worth while. Patient waiters are never losers.

Some conflicts are so controversial that agreements are very hard to keep. If this kind of agreement fails, you should assume that it will take several cycles of debate to achieve a solution. Controversial issues can include:

- legacy anger – a carry over of hostility by people who were not part of the original conflict; loyalty to ancient memory makes them want to fight
- severe losses – the desire to recover money, property, pride or health
- perceived unfairness of the voting system
- corruption in the debating process
- extreme inequality in the debaters' skill levels.

Putting it all together

The purpose of debate is to allow an independent audience to consider different points of view. This gives the conflicting sides a chance to reach a conclusion – usually based on the vote of the independents. Debate doesn't and can't end hostility, but it can support a fair outcome by providing a framework for a full and frank discussion. Even when debaters are combative, show anger and make brutal remarks, they know that when they finish the other side has an equal chance to tear into them.

This awareness helps keep the proceedings civilized. Debate is a way to allow differences to be expressed, acknowledged and accepted. These differences can actually support harmony for the long term so that everyone benefits. This contrasts with the kind of peace that buries resentment and depends on pretending that conflict doesn't exist. In this situation it's only a matter of time before it all erupts again, so the pretence does more harm than good to all sides.

37 GIVE PEOPLE A SECOND CHANCE

'Resentment is like drinking poison and then hoping it will kill your enemies.'
Nelson Mandela

'The weak can never forgive. Forgiveness is the attribute of the strong.'
Mahatma Gandhi

'Holding on to anger, resentment and hurt only gives you tense muscles, a headache and a sore jaw from clenching your teeth. Forgiveness gives you back the laughter and the lightness in your life.'
Joan Lunden

'Forgiveness says you are given another chance to make a new beginning.'
Desmond Tutu

'We all have big changes in our lives that are more or less a second chance.'
Harrison Ford

What is a second chance? Is it an opportunity to correct a mistake, ask forgiveness or start again with the past erased? Examples of second chances from politics at the end of the twentieth century include peace-seeking initiatives among nations troubled by civil war. These were 'second-chance movements' because the warring parties were asked to put aside their differences and try again. This occurred most famously in South Africa under Nelson Mandela, but also in Northern Ireland, Bosnia and, most recently, in Burma.

Usually referred to as reconciliation, the goal was learning to get along, accept and live with differences. It didn't say 'forgive and forget'. This would have been too great a leap. Instead, each of the warring parties had to acknowledge past behaviour and make a commitment not to repeat it. This approach recognized that fear, mistrust and hatred do not simply disappear, but that people cannot bear living for ever with such terrible negativity. Their only realistic option is to give and receive a second chance and make a new beginning.

In business, it's also necessary to start again on occasion. Mutual dependence can force an arm's-length acceptance of another side's behaviour. The banking crisis of 2008 onwards is a good example. Because the general public needed banking services, people had to carry on using a dysfunctional banking system as governments around the world acted to prop up the failing industry. Although banking leaders of that time are unlikely ever to be forgiven, the public's need of banks made reconciliation necessary.

This wary acceptance of banking and bankers by the public also reveals the why, when and how of giving a second chance. Another chance must, or seemingly will always, be granted when parties need each other to survive, provide mutual benefit, feel whole, or share values. By contrast, when a relationship is transitory and there is little to gain from working together, a second chance may be a mistake.

This secret is about deciding when to give a second chance because there is always someone in need of one. Human beings make mistakes. Some are so terrible that they can't be forgiven, but the people who made them may still need to receive a second chance. The issue is to know when it's a good idea and when it's not.

STOP INVASION AND AVOID ESCALATION

Robert Axelrod, in his book *The Evolution of Cooperation*, describes how he organized one of the first computer tournaments in the 1980s. His goal was to discover what made co-operation possible in a world dominated by self-interest and lacking any assurance of fairness. This tournament led Axelrod to suggest that there are three guiding principles that lead to co-operation in general:

1. Always give back what you get. This means that when someone withdraws support, you immediately withdraw yours without exception.
2. Return to co-operation as soon as the other person becomes co-operative again. Mirroring the other person prevents them from invading your territory and stops you from escalating the conflict.
3. Never be the first one to withhold co-operation.

The tournament was organized into rounds, with each player going against all the others in turn. The object was to guess whether the others would co-operate, and collect points based on whether these guesses were accurate. The winner was the game that scored the most points. The games that lasted longest always began with a move to co-operate. In contrast, the games that led with non-cooperative behaviour were quickly eliminated.

The ultimate winner was a game called Tit for Tat. This game always returned the behaviour of the opposing game. If the opposing game attacked, Tit for Tat did the same. If it became co-operative, so did Tit for Tat.

BE READY TO CO-OPERATE WHEN ASKED

Axelrod discovered that all the non-cooperative games got knocked out of play very fast. They not only lost against the other non-cooperators, but also against the co-operators that practised payback. Payback was a rule that made co-operating games fight back when attacked. But it also allowed a player to return to forgiveness if the opponent wanted to co-operate again.

The eventual winner, Tit for Tat, was the game that immediately retaliated when it was attacked and with equal speed returned to co-operate when its opponent did. Tit for Tat also had what Axelrod called a forgiveness rule, or a second-chance rule. This is counter-intuitive if you believe that being tough and the first to attack is a necessity in business. A few years later this computer tournament was repeated, with many of the same players. Tit for Tat won again, showing that it does pay to co-operate.

However, when colleagues are substance abusers, chronically late, always absent or even have their hand in the till, unlimited forgiveness doesn't work. But you can say yes to the first request for a second chance. Agreeing to this is a safe bet. But if they let you down again, practise Tit for Tat and withdraw all support.

At work this can't go on indefinitely. There comes a point when there have been too many disappointments, and you have to cut the person off. However, be prepared to give yet another chance if later the person seems to have changed and there is mutual benefit to forgiveness.

EVALUATE EACH SITUATION

The computer tournament shows that the first move should be co-operation, that is, give a second chance. But what do you do when the same person makes a second mistake? Instinct says to refuse to forgive. However, people are complex and so are the situations they create.

Here is a checklist to help you decide what to do. If you answer yes to any of the statements, then it's probably a good idea to give a second chance.

- Environmental influences led to the mistake:
  - The work location's physical features caused unforeseen problems. ☐
  - There were unhelpful colleagues or a lack of necessary support. ☐
- Differences in background, culture and language led to misunderstanding the rules or misinterpreting their importance. ☐
- You have a long-standing relationship with the person and know that there are hidden factors that caused the mistake. ☐

- Performance has improved since the last mistake and further progress is likely. ☐
- The person is a giver, a positive person who brings intangible benefits to the working group. ☐
- The person has taken full responsibility for past mistakes. ☐
- There is honesty and directness in all your dealings with this person. ☐
- Colleagues who work closely with the person recommend another chance. ☐

Putting it all together

Deciding to give a second chance is one of the hardest things a leader has to do. It takes compassion to forgive and patience to listen to the explanation about what went wrong. Good judgement is needed to discover whether the person is truly sorry and determined not to repeat the mistake. But even if you possess all three qualities, you can still find it very difficult to decide about giving a second chance.

People are so complex that predicting who will change for the better, and who will not, is impossible. But this means that it's a better choice to give the second chance than refuse the request. This is because you can never know which choice is correct, and so err on the side of forgiveness.

However, you also know in business that the number of second chances available has to be limited. When you give this, it's important to let the person know that it's a very serious matter. An easy-going attitude risks giving people the idea that you forgive easily, and are not really disappointed or upset by the behaviour. In terms of Tit for Tat, this risks allowing invasion.

38 LEARN FROM EVERYONE AND EVERYTHING

'Education is the ability to listen to almost anything without losing your temper or your self-confidence.'
Robert Frost

'Leadership and learning are indispensable to each other.'
John F. Kennedy

'Everything that irritates us about others can lead us to an understanding of ourselves.'
Carl G. Jung

'I never teach my pupils; I only attempt to provide the conditions in which they can learn.'
Albert Einstein

'I am learning all the time. The tombstone will be my diploma.'
Eartha Kitt

Educated people always want to learn more. They are never satisfied with what they already know because their current interests push them to study further. This in turn increases their ideas so that they need to study even more. This is fun for them and they create a virtuous circle of learning – all for its own sake. Credentials, diplomas, certificates or degrees are extras, not the real purpose of education. They have too many questions in need of answers to think about pieces of paper.

Leaders need this quality and a desire to understand the world around them. The sum of knowledge increases daily, as well as universal access to it through technology, and so they need to keep up with this. Sometimes traditional learning isn't enough and so an openness to unconventional education creates further learning opportunities.

Anyone and anything can introduce new knowledge. Children at infant school are now taught to filter information so that they create their own learning plans using specifically designed apps. There are hundreds of opportunities that feature specific regions, topics and people for study. These opportunities allow customized learning.

One definition of learning is 'the acquisition or increase of knowledge, behaviour, skill, values or ideas through exposure to experience'. Another includes the idea that it's a process that takes place over time. Learning can also be analysed. Some educators suggest making a graph of the learning process, with 'Learning' placed on the vertical or y-axis and 'Timing' on the horizontal or x-axis.

Musical training lends itself to plotting on a graph like this. It requires hours of practice to develop hand–eye co-ordination, and so results in a gently rising learning curve. By contrast, bungee jumping requires a short burst of very intense training, and so its graph is a sharply rising line. Learning charts help teachers and students alike to manage expectations for the time needed to study before any results may be shown. This avoids frustration and a lack of realism about what can be achieved within a certain timeframe.

A learning graph can also be flat with no curve at all – just a straight line showing that time passed without any learning. Examples include:

- students who attend school but never learn to read or write
- travellers who visit exotic countries but stay in a tour group to avoid contact with local people and customs
- business executives who attend leadership courses, but ignore what's presented because they already know the answers.

USE EXPERIENCE TO INCREASE LEARNING

Daniel Kolb is a psychologist who believes that learning should ideally occur in four stages. The first stage begins with a new experience. This is followed by a time-out stage to think about that experience and to identify both good and bad results. The third stage builds on this with decisions about what to do differently next time. The final stage practises the new ideas that were identified in stage three.

This four-stage model promotes continuous learning based on action and experience. Its focus on reflection and deciding how to do better next time is practical and leads to rapid learning. However, Kolb also suggests that experiential learning needs certain skills and qualities. These are:

- willingness to study the experience
- ability to observe yourself in action and think about what you do as you do it
- analytical skill to think about your experience, towards improving it next time
- commitment to act on the improvements in future.

IDENTIFY HOW YOU LEARN

It's a good idea to know how you learn. For example, do you prefer studying alone or in a group? If alone, then you are likely to benefit from online learning or digital courses. However, if you prefer face-to-face interaction with a teacher, debating new ideas with colleagues, or getting immediate feedback from other people in a training situation, then signing up for an instructed course will help you more.

One way to identify which kind of experience works better for you is to try using a teach-yourself DVD. Ask yourself whether you feel frustrated by its structured approach or have questions that need answering before you can proceed to further modules. If so, you are likely to benefit more from interaction with others.

Alternatively, if it's difficult for you to concentrate in a group or you find that the content moves too slowly or too quickly for you in this kind of learning situation, you're likely to gain more from working alone.

Once you know the kind of situation that supports the way you learn, you can consider your learning style. There are three main styles:

1. **Visual:** using images, video, colour and shapes
2. **Aural:** using voice for singing, speech for reading aloud and vocal explanations
3. **Manual:** using your hands and doing physical activity

Although you will probably use all three styles, you may prefer one more than the others.

LOOK FOR OPPORTUNITIES TO LEARN

Books, courses and teachers in classrooms all offer opportunities to learn. However, casual meetings, remarks heard on the news or elsewhere can open the way to seeing the world differently. You need only be prepared for the experience.

- **Past – is there anything you always wanted to learn?**
  Is there a musical instrument, a foreign language, a hobby or sport that you have always wanted to study, do or explore, but never had the time? Think of ways you can pursue one of these ideas. If this is unrealistic, identify a substitute that is doable and will offer a new experience.

- **Present – break your routine and be curious**
  A busy lifestyle offers little time for curiosity or the opportunity to make new connections and find creative solutions. Routines become more rigid as time pressure increases. An antidote is to take a different route to work or leave a bit earlier than usual so that you can walk part of the way and find a place to sit and think. Let your thoughts drift and reflect on your life without judging or worrying about the results.

Very busy and time-pressured people may protest, 'Where am I going to get the time to leave a bit earlier in the morning?' If this is you, then cut one thing from your early-morning routine. Change one thing and gain a few extra minutes for reflection time or just reading. You need this.

- **Future – learn something together with a family member or friend**
Studying or training with a friend or family member changes your learning experience entirely. It allows you to see the topic or activity through their eyes as well as your own. Having their company also makes your learning more enjoyable.

Putting it all together

Everything that happens can be a source of new knowledge, as long as there's time to reflect on what happened and to decide how to apply any new understanding to real-life situations. Learning is a lifetime activity. When entering an area where you have little or no experience, create a learning programme.

Make a rough diagram of what your learning curve would be like. This can help you manage expectations about the speed of your learning. Plotting a learning curve in advance shows what progress can be made in an ideal situation. If actual progress fails to match your learning plan, you can decide either to increase your practice or change the curve because it doesn't work for you with this subject. Either way, you avoid feeling discouraged.

When you have an open mind to new ideas, you increase productivity because solutions to complex problems emerge naturally while you focus on other things. Learning as a way of life gives you access to a vast storeroom of information in the back of your mind. It becomes available when you need it. All you need to do is take time to reflect – and there it is. (Refer also to Secret 49, *Have a big idea*.)

39 SET TARGETS FOR PERSONAL GROWTH

'We could never learn to be brave and patient if there were only joy in the world.'
Helen Keller

'It isn't normal to know what we want. It is a rare and difficult psychological achievement.'
Abraham Maslow

'Don't be afraid to give your best to what seemingly are small jobs. Every time you conquer one it makes you that much stronger. If you do the little jobs well, the big ones will tend to take care of themselves.'
Dale Carnegie

'Give yourself something to work toward constantly.'
Mary Kay Ash

'A mind that is stretched by a new experience can never go back to its old dimensions.'
Oliver Wendell Holmes, Jr.

It seems to be part of the human DNA to find ways to develop and grow. The drive to experience extreme sports, enter a pub quiz or study at night after work comes from the same impulse – a wish to be better and know more. For some, this drive is focused. They know exactly what they want to learn and how to go about it. For others, it's more difficult to decide what they want and how to develop.

Personal growth means different things to different people because people grow in line with their individual values and priorities. Athletes want to improve their performance; students want to study and gain knowledge; politicians want to use influence and gain power. Everyone wants to grow in ways that achieve their personal goals. And everyone has potential to make a unique contribution to their communities in a blend of skills, qualities and ideas that produce a one-off human being.

Personal goals are also influenced by cultural values. Aristotle, a major influence on Western thinking, emphasized living a balanced life and making the pursuit of social values and community spirit a priority. In the East, Confucius linked personal development to supporting the family so that individual talent would benefit the whole unit. The great world religions also suggest that personal development should serve society.

Andrew Carnegie, a leading American industrialist in the nineteenth century and one of the world's great philanthropists, began life in extreme poverty. Living in a city slum, he got his first job at 13, but soon learned that he could borrow one book a week from a local dignitary who opened his private library every Saturday morning. This allowed the young Andrew to educate himself.

No matter how tired he would be after a 12-hour shift, he would read and study. Whenever he found an opportunity to increase his skills and knowledge, he took it. By the time he was 30, he had already created his first fortune. As his wealth increased, he opened libraries and founded schools to encourage young people to educate themselves. His own drive to develop his potential made him believe this was possible for everyone else. They only needed determination to succeed.

WAKE UP EARLY

Time management experts advise waking up early to work on achieving your goals before other people's priorities take over. Even 15 minutes makes a difference if you use the time to decide what's important to you. Although it can be tempting to update posts, check emails, or watch a new grumpy cat video, this time should be set aside to think about what you want in your life. And every minute counts.

Abraham Maslow, a pioneering psychologist from the twentieth century, is quoted above as saying, 'It isn't normal to know what we want.' This may explain why so many people lack personal goals and a plan to achieve them. Your 15 minutes in the morning can help you decide how the day ahead can meet your goals for personal and professional growth. If you don't have any goals as yet, this should signal to you how important it is for you to get started right away.

Begin by asking yourself what you want in your life in five years' time in areas of family, home, work, money, health and friends. Think about this in terms of:

- what you already have
- what you like about it
- what's missing.

You can actually start your 15-minute growth plan the night before, by considering what you want to think about during your 15 minutes. Think about this while getting ready for bed or just before you go to sleep. By preparing your mind, it will be easier to get started when you wake up.

MAKE A BUCKET LIST

Knowing what targets you want to achieve is a challenge. You need to decide what you want in your life now, as well as what you may want in the future – although you don't yet know the people you'll meet, where you'll go, what films you'll see or books you'll read. You also have no idea what influences will occur in your life. This can make deciding your learning targets very difficult, especially if you live day to day without thinking about your future.

But recognizing that you don't know what you want can be as much a positive as it is a negative because it gives you the chance to think about your real priorities – that is, what's most important to you right now. You get to start with a clean piece of paper and make a bucket list. This is a list of all the things you want to do before you die. It comes from 'kick the bucket', a slang expression meaning to die.

It's best to let your imagination run freely when making this list. Avoid deciding too soon that one idea is better than another. Think of people you've always admired and ask yourself what you would like to copy that they do. Ask yourself whether there is a feeling or quality you've always wanted in your life, and then think what you could do to experience that feeling. Add to the list as you think of things to do. This list can become another source of targets for your personal growth.

MAKE LEARNING A PRIORITY

Formal education is fine for people who like studying in a classroom, have good schools and teachers available, and believe that it leads somewhere. But not everyone fits into these categories. Bill Gates, the richest man in the world, famously never finished his university degree. Instead, he spent his time at Harvard using its computer laboratory to develop the code that later made his fortune.

He doesn't regret his decision to drop out, and he even jokes about it. By contrast, Ada Smith is an elegant 50-year-old who left school without qualifications. She feels embarrassed that she never got a university degree and secretly believes she isn't smart enough to get one. Entirely self-taught, she has financial expertise that draws high-net-worth clients seeking her investment advice, all of whom are attracted by word-of-mouth recommendation.

This is strange, but people often want what they believe they can't have, making it even more important to follow a dream and set targets for personal growth. Here's a checklist to get you started:

1. Decide on a topic that interests you. ☐
2. Investigate the way this is taught in a formal education setting. ☐
3. Refer to Secret 38, *Learn from everything and everyone,* and identify your learning style. ☐
4. Think about what you want to learn and estimate the time you need to make progress (see Secret 38). ☐

5. Collect all the learning materials you need together in one place. ☐
6. Put time aside on a regular basis to learn your topic. ☐
7. Keep going even through the boring parts – *especially* through the boring parts. ☐

Putting it all together

Personal development begins with an attitude, a feeling of possibility, and a decision to stretch beyond your present circumstances. This applies equally to those with family responsibilities or special circumstances that limit their ability to change careers or increase formal education. Growth is more difficult but it's still possible – as shown by the great number of self-made men and women who started out with nothing but worked slowly and steadily to meet their goals.

Education is the key to achieving targets, but this means so much more than going to school, college or university. It's a wish to know things for their own sake and add to understanding to enrich your life. At its best, it's entirely self-directed and determined. Mental freedom results from this kind of education, and provides the basis for an unassailable self-confidence.

40 ASK FOR HELP WHEN YOU NEED IT

'The best thing to do when you find yourself in a hurting or vulnerable place is to surround yourself with the strongest, finest, most positive people you know.'
Kristin Armstrong

'Refusing to ask for help when you need it is refusing someone the chance to be helpful.'
Ric Ocasek

'You are never strong enough that you don't need help.'
Cesar Chavez

'No one who achieves success does so without acknowledging the help of others. The wise and confident acknowledge this help with gratitude.'
Alfred North Whitehead

'When we give cheerfully and accept gratefully, everyone is blessed.'
Maya Angelou

Pride is healthy when it supports high standards, offers a guide to performance, and inspires others to do their best. 'Bursting with pride' describes the feeling of watching friends or family winning an award or facing difficult challenges successfully. It's also the feeling of quiet joy that follows winning after making serious personal effort. Having this kind of pride makes it easy to ask for help as well as to acknowledge receiving it.

But pride can also stop people from asking for help. In this case it's not a virtue at all, but a form of self-protection and a reaction to feeling vulnerable. This is an isolated place to be, and often the only way to escape is to ask for help. Ironically, however, having too much negative pride makes this very difficult. The more cut off a person feels, the more difficult it is to reach out to other people.

This is also a very dangerous place for leaders to be because people depend on them. If they become trapped in unhealthy pride, everyone suffers. Although there are many reasons for leaders not to ask for help, those that can result from pride include:

- fear of being exploited after admitting vulnerability
- loss of face and status when shifting from giving to needing to receive
- risk of humiliation and embarrassment if their request is rejected.

There are some truly unpleasant people out there who would happily take advantage of those who are vulnerable, and so these are legitimate concerns. Leaders must balance meeting immediate needs with long-term reputation and position. To this end, there are steps that can maintain status and minimize the appearance of vulnerability:

1. Decide exactly what kind of help is necessary to solve which specific problem and for what duration of time.
2. Frame the problem in positive terms. Change 'We can't pay our bills' to 'We need a specific amount of cash for a defined reason to be repaid by a certain date.'
3. Identify someone who is now in position of strength who once experienced a similar problem.
4. Ask for advice and help, but with an offer of some special service in return.

KNOW WHEN TO ASK FOR HELP

Credit counsellors, human resource psychologists and medical doctors all report that many people don't ask for help when they need it. They quietly and desperately hang on to what they think is their dignity while sinking ever deeper into difficulty.

In competitive or hostile environments, they actively hide a need for help. In families, they keep illness or failure a secret to save others from worry.

But problems very rarely go away by themselves. The sufferer needs first to acknowledge that they need help and then take action to get it. Here are some examples of situations that show it's time to ask for help:

- You block any thought of the problem and escape from further reference to it by any means available.
- You regularly imagine losing control of the problem and being forced to take action you disagree with or believe is unnecessary.
- You avoid seeing the people who can help you, although you also pray that they'll discover your difficulties and offer to rescue you.
- You wake up feeling as if you are drowning. You feel dizzy all day.

These symptoms may help you think of more. Everyone has been there – absolutely everyone – even the strongest and the best – everyone. Certainly, every leader who has ever faced a crisis has been there. As soon as a situation causes even one negative reaction, it's best to find an independent source of help and describe the problem.

SAY THANK YOU

After asking for help, the next step is saying thank you. Amazingly, this doesn't always happen. Even gracious, pleasant and well-mannered people can forget to let others know how much they value their help. It's a mistake to think that saying thanks isn't necessary among friends, or that an emergency situation or time pressures makes it OK to neglect the courtesy. Whatever the situation, the words 'Thank you' must be said.

Expressing gratitude is essential and reinforces the bond between giver and receiver.

Failure to do this can be damaging, both to the receiver's reputation and to their chance of receiving help in future. People want to be appreciated and anyone who does a service out of kindness or even as a paid professional deserves this. It's an uncomfortable feeling to give and then hear nothing back.

The ungrateful are rightly labelled arrogant, entitled, boorish and rude. Unfortunately, those who rarely ask for help, and then only on one occasion forget to say thanks, risk being bundled with those who ignore the courtesy repeatedly. This can seem unfair, but lack of appreciation hurts. Whether help consisted of money, time, listening, advice or something else, 'Thank you' must be said.

CALL IN FAVOURS REGULARLY

Some people are always prepared to ask for help. They certainly don't need any tips on how to do this. Rather, they could write a book called *How I Get Other People to Do My Work*. If unchecked, these colleagues will sit idle while getting you to act for them. However, saying no when you are asked for help can seem petty, particularly if the request is for something small. This is compounded when the request for help is made in public. Then you not only feel petty; you actually look it as well.

One way to check this behaviour is by identifying a few catchphrases to use when asked to run errands, do menial tasks, or act as an unpaid servant. The goal is to discourage being asked in future. If used and reused faithfully, catchphrases can help you achieve this.

For example, you may be asked to pick up a colleague's dry cleaning on your way back from lunch. It's easier to refuse if you have a catchphrase ready. Here are three samples that can be varied with each situation:

1. 'I'd love to do you a favour, but I can't today. Ask me another time, for sure.'
2. 'Thanks for asking. Not today, and you still owe for the coffee from yesterday.'
3. 'I don't have time, but will you please organize those project notes from yesterday?'

Furthermore

You need to call in favours on a regular basis. Avoid being the person who helps but asks for nothing in return. This is not generous; it's unhealthy and undermines your professional credibility. When a colleague asks for help, you can of course agree to this if it's appropriate. But add that you'd like their support as well, and be ready to name a project. Even if you don't ask for help later, you've made it clear that you want reciprocity, either now or in the future.

Putting it all together

Asking for help is a skill well worth acquiring. It's as important as knowing how, when and what to give. Animals, especially primates, show both giving and receiving skills when they groom each other. First, one combs the other's fur or feathers, removing debris and tangles, then the other takes a turn.

Grooming animals assume that there will be reciprocity and are pretty sure they will get this. This is because animals who fail to return the favour risk never getting groomed again, and also because no animal denies itself the feel-good chemicals they get when giving grooming as well as when receiving it. Scientists have taken blood samples from pairs of animals before, during and after grooming and found that grooming releases beta-endorphins, a chemical that causes relaxation and feelings of pleasure.

Accepting help does create vulnerability, but this can be a good thing. Macho, ultra-independent people – both men and women – need to rethink the benefits of doing everything themselves. Yes, it's impressive that they did it all alone, but the question is why, when they could have had some help.

41 SET AN EXAMPLE

'There are two ways of spreading light: to be the candle, or to be the mirror that reflects it.'
Edith Wharton

'The older I get the less I listen to what people say and the more I look at what they do.'
Andrew Carnegie

'If Rosa Parks had taken a poll before she sat down in the bus in Montgomery, she'd still be standing.'
Mary Frances Berry

'I try to lead by example.'
Usain Bolt

'There is no power on earth that can neutralize the influence of a high, simple, and useful life.'
Booker T. Washington

Children learn to speak by listening to people talking and then imitating the sounds. Left alone, they practise the sounds – 'bah-bah-bah-oo-ah-dah' – until eventually they manage to say their first word, more by accident than intention. They learn by watching, listening and copying the older members of the family. But copying is often done unconsciously. This is why careful parents want their children to have wholesome friends so that the habits they share will keep them out of trouble.

Unfortunately, troublemakers can look attractive, and following their example may seem more fun. There's a lesson in this for leaders. It isn't enough to set an example. This works only if people want to follow it. If a leader lacks influence or credibility, or has an unattractive personality, it's more likely that the example will be ridiculed or mistrusted.

However, setting an example is a great way to encourage everyone to follow rules, accept standards of behaviour and use the right processes and procedures. When the boss comes in early every day, it's harder for others to arrive late. When the team leader uses a discount airline, it's difficult for anyone seeing this to justify booking a business-class flight. When information is shared openly, hostile gossip and back-stabbing disappear.

Setting an example works well when the behaviour is clearly aligned to business success. People like to know why an example is relevant and what purpose it serves. When a tiger teaches her cubs to hunt, they know the purpose is to catch their dinner. She lines them up at a safe distance from the prey to watch until she captures it. She does this several times before taking them in turn to hunt alongside her. Next, she sends them out together, to hunt as a pack.

Gradually, they learn the necessary skills to hunt alone. Because the cubs want to survive, they have a drive to learn to hunt. In a similar way, when leaders want new guidelines or better standards to be accepted, they first should explain why they are important and then show by example that it's necessary to follow them, in both letter and spirit.

EXPLAIN WHY YOU DO WHAT YOU DO

Every day Angelica Forrest goes to the cafeteria to pick up her lunch. She has a liver disorder and needs to avoid certain fatty foods. When she joined the firm six months earlier, she met with the cafeteria manager and arranged to pay by the month an extra amount for special lunches. It's expensive but it saves her time in the morning and ensures that she keeps to her diet.

The company staff all use the cafeteria, including, of course, Angelica's own team. Prices are generally low and everyone appreciates the subsidy. However, there's growing resentment of Angelica. People see her breeze in early every day to collect her lunch, ready-made and waiting for her in the cold cabinet. She never pays; she doesn't even carry money.

Angelica has no idea how her new colleagues interpret her behaviour. If she knew, she'd be horrified. She actually believes that no one notices her when she pops into the cafeteria as early as she can get there. Little does she know that her carefully controlled and entirely boring lunch has taken on a fabulous level of importance, with imagined sandwich fillings of smoked salmon, coronation chicken and other treats.

Fixing this situation is easy. Just once a week she should join her own team at a cafeteria table, open her lunch bag, and say how boring it is to have exactly the same lunch every day. This would allow her to explain her daily lunch pick-up and drop a hint about the cost. She should finish the story with reference to its saving a few precious minutes in the morning when she needs to drop the children at school and her elderly mother at the community centre. The gossip would simply stop.

MAKE YOUR BEHAVIOUR EASY TO COPY

Think of a leader you admire and ask yourself why you admire them. Is it their behaviour, an attitude or a way of speaking that you think is worthy of respect? Or maybe the way that person lives makes you to want to do or be the same. Now consider how you know about it: whether it's through news coverage, the Internet, a film or a book. Somehow that leader's story reached you and inspired you.

When setting an example, you need to let everyone know the story behind it, why it's important, and also exactly what you think should be copied. Your example has to be clear and understandable without any guesswork. In Angelica's case, she risked setting a negative example without knowing it. Her colleagues imagined that she was dishonestly getting a free lunch. This kind of morale buster can create a negative example and lead to petty dishonesty and poor co-operation.

To make it easy for people to follow your example, break it into segments. It may be something you do so often yourself that analysing it is a challenge, so first decide its most important feature. For example, if you want the team to increase client contact, you need to explain what kind of contact is needed and to what purpose. Next, point out occasions when you noticed they did this well. Finally, suggest that they refine their skills by watching you or another skilled person.

BE THE BEST YOU CAN BE

At times, the simple act of saying yes or no can change history. Rosa Parks is an example of an American hero from the Civil Rights Movement during the second half of the twentieth century. A modest and unassuming woman, she stepped into this role one evening when riding the bus home from her work as a seamstress in an Alabama factory.

Buses at that time in Alabama were divided into two sections, with white people seated at the front and African Americans at the back. Although white passengers could sit anywhere, African Americans were limited to the rear seats. However, when all the white section seats became filled, the bus driver could demand that an African American give up his or her seat.

This happened to Rosa Parks on 1 December 1955. But when the driver told her to give up her seat so that a white male could take it, she refused. Later she explained, 'I had been pushed as far as I could stand.' As a result, she was arrested for breaking the segregation laws and instantly became the figurehead for a boycott of the bus service that lasted 381 days. Her action eventually led to repeal of segregation laws.

Deciding to be the best you can be on a daily basis means being prepared to making a tough choice when under fire. Rosa Parks was an ordinary person who took a heroic stand. Her example changed history.

Putting it all together

Descriptions of famous leaders usually include examples of how they behaved at turning points in their lives. Wartime heroes are an example, with their acts of bravery inspiring courage and strength in those who hear their stories. Although copying their behaviour is impossible in everyday life, ordinary people can imitate the attitude and the qualities they expressed.

There are so many examples of quiet courage as families struggle to pay bills, get their children to school, go to work, and somehow find time to care for elderly relatives or neighbours who need help. These are examples of fortitude and kindness as well.

Setting an example works if you make it clear what you want copied and if you can convince people that it's worth the effort for them to imitate you. Link the example to shared values, a common cause or a necessary achievement. This makes it a professional choice to copy specific behaviour. Individualistic and independent people can dislike the idea of copying other people, but they are often willing to copy specific behaviour if it serves the right purpose.

42 WATCH OUT – YOU'RE BEING WATCHED

'There are four ways, and only four ways, in which we have contact with the world. We are evaluated and classified by these four contacts: what we do, how we look, what we say, and how we say it.'

Dale Carnegie

'Big Brother is watching you.'
Slogan of the totalitarian state in
George Orwell's Nineteen Eighty-four

'I've studied pathological liars, and anything they say, they believe, and that's one of the reasons they're so convincing, because they have no connection with the truth. It's a dead issue. It's like they're colour-blind to the truth. So anything that comes out of their mouths is their reality.'

Jane Velez-Mitchell

'Whenever you do a thing, act as if all the world were watching.'

Thomas Jefferson

'I saw a crow building a nest, I was watching him very carefully, I was kind of stalking him and he was aware of it. And you know what they do when they become aware of someone stalking them when they build a nest, which is a very vulnerable place to be? They build a decoy nest. It's just for you.'

Tom Waits

Leaders live in a goldfish bowl and the amount they are watched increases with their importance. The previous secret, 41, *Set an example*, refers to occasions when leaders want and choose to be watched. They're driven by an educational purpose and have control over the situation. This isn't the case with this secret: this is about being watched without consent, approval or even awareness that it's taking place, and those new to leadership can feel overwhelmed when they discover it's happening to them.

Leaders who dislike the idea of being watched need to discover how to retain their privacy while being in the public eye. This, like everything else, requires balance. Those who build a wall between themselves and others – even justifiably, to protect themselves and their family – risk cutting themselves off from their colleagues. If they also withdraw from public scrutiny this can create an impression that they have something to hide.

Neither idea is good. It's also not such a good idea to build a decoy life, as described in the Tom Waits' quote about crows. These solutions – if they can be called this – dehumanize rather than protect and should be avoided. The better, if also unattractive solution, is just to accept that being watched is a part of modern life and certainly of modern leadership. And it's also not at all a new situation in community life.

Anyone who has ever lived in a small town or village knows that privacy doesn't exist and that nosiness is normal in closed communities. When the telephone was first invented, local operators listened to all the calls and became the best sources of gossip. No leader would have been spared. Those with servants had their every word and deed reported to anyone who would listen. Because there were fewer leaders, the scrutiny would have been even more severe.

The migration from country to city offered a welcome anonymity for many at that time. Ironically, more privacy can now be found in the country. Fewer people live there and tight communal links have broken down. Houses are behind walls and Internet shopping allows purchasing in private. There may, in due course, be a reverse exodus from city to country. But those leaders who are hungry for more privacy may be missing the point. It's their job to be watched. They are people of interest, even if they don't want to be. It's part of the price they pay to lead.

WATCH THE WATCHERS

The UK has one surveillance camera in a public place for every 14 people. It's also estimated that 20 per cent of the world's cameras are watching the UK public. In the United States there are around 30 million surveillance cameras and, although the courts strictly monitor violations of privacy in that country, there's no law governing public video capture at the time of this writing.

Watching just grows without any checks, and for the most part no one complains. This is somewhat surprising. Scientists from the University of Sydney recently announced that one of the brain's most primitive functions is to stay alert to being watched and therefore awake to the danger of attack. Surveillance cameras are inert recorders of events and entirely impersonal, and so maybe this primal part of our brain ignores or doesn't notice them.

For whatever reason, people generally forget that they are being watched 24/7 whenever they go out for a bottle of milk or a loaf of bread. But leaders do need to be aware, and more cautious and conscious of the image they project. Being dignified, or at least clean and neat, whenever they are in public are basics. They also need to be aware of respecting privacy laws themselves when installing cameras in the workplace.

When is it right and appropriate to record events, and when is it an invasion of privacy? What kind of warnings should be made that surveillance takes place? What are employee rights to privacy both in national law and in the organization's rulebook? Having answers to these questions ensures best practice.

ACT AS IF THE CAMERA IS ON YOU

A famous film star recently said in an interview that, whenever she goes into public places, she imagines being watched by someone who has a crush on her. It's her way of dealing with press invasion and the need to be aware that she can be filmed anywhere, at any time. When asked whether she found this demanding and unfair, she answered that she chose to have a public life and so accepts the attention as part of that choice.

It can't be comfortable, though, and this is the dark side of social media and digital imaging. Anyone with a phone camera can take a high-value picture of a celebrity and make money from it. Leaders from every area of life need to think about this as well. Any civil servant who argues angrily with a sales clerk can become newsworthy to the local press, and a local dignitary can be photographed parking illegally in a space reserved for the disabled.

But feelings of being watched do lead to greater honesty. In a study from the University of Newcastle upon Tyne, placing an image of a pair of eyes next to the honesty box in a university coffee room led to people paying nearly three times as much for drinks as those in a control group.

BE AWARE OF POLITICS

As a leader you attract envy, with complete strangers wanting your job, your desk or even your files. Their motives range from a wish for your status and power, the admiration you attract or your salary. Anyone who has actually held a leadership role knows that, no matter how high you are on the food chain, there's always someone higher who has more power. Even the CEO answers to a board of directors or shareholders.

As for admiration, it's more likely that you get a daily kicking from anyone who wants to have a go, and the salary is never enough for what you have to do for it. But anyone not in your job may well imagine it is a Xanadu of delight. It's why they want you out and themselves in your office chair. This category of watchers can endanger your security because they are less interested in accuracy than those who have commissioned the installation of a surveillance camera. Envious people want to discover a fault, however small, that will show you in a bad light. Their watching, as a result, is relentless and unforgiving.

Furthermore

Transparency and excellent communication skills save a leader who has to endure political scrambling of this kind. Make it clear why you do what you do, and how you chose to do it. As you progress in your career, creating a paper trail should become effortless and automatic. It will also help you stay scrupulously honest when under stress.

Putting it all together

Being watched when in a pubic place is a strange idea, but it's also increasingly the case. The current situation developed so gradually that there was never a single moment when anyone could say 'Ouch!' loudly enough for it to matter. It's like the story of the frog in a pan of cold water. If you put it on the fire, the water heats so gradually that the frog doesn't realize it's being cooked and so it doesn't jump out.

However, the average, law-abiding citizen believes that cameras keep the streets safe, and any loss of personal privacy is a small price to pay for this protection. And as long as those managing the recordings are benign, this may be correct. But for leaders it's crucially important that they are always aware that they can be watched.

On the positive side, behaving well in public is just another discipline in an already structured life. It's also a help to avoid any grey area of behaviour. As the University of Newcastle research showed, having a watching pair of eyes on them kept students honest.

43 CHOOSE A LEADERSHIP STYLE

'Anyone can hold the helm when the sea is calm.'
Publilius Syrus

'Companies used to be able to function with autocratic bosses. We don't live in that world anymore.'
Rosabeth Moss Kanter

'The best executive is the one who has sense enough to pick good people to do what needs to be done, and self-restraint to keep from meddling with them while they do it.'
Theodore Roosevelt

'I am more afraid of an army of 100 sheep led by a lion than an army of 100 lions led by a sheep.'
Charles Maurice de Talleyrand-Périgord (Talleyrand)

'At one time leadership meant muscle; but today it means getting along with people.'
Indira Gandhi

Skilled leaders adapt to changing situations. They both consciously and unconsciously alter their behaviour as necessary in order to bring people together in a spirit of goodwill to achieve a common goal. They learn to do this by interacting with all kinds of people, in a range of weird and wonderful situations. Over time, it becomes second nature for them to assess their circumstances and behave accordingly.

Norman Schwarzkopf was an American general responsible for many military campaigns. Nicknamed 'Stormin' Norman', he is an example of a highly decorated officer as famous for his fiery temper and purposeful demands as for his military diplomacy and much admired by those who served under him. When in command of a major military operation he could seamlessly move from a heated discussion with his staff to a press briefing that gave clear, comprehensive and concise updates and reports.

Schwarzkopf had skill as an adaptable leader in a job usually stereotyped as suitable for more rigid personalities. However, his overall excellence is rare. Many leaders show more skill in one area than another, with most lacking the ability to adapt quickly when moving from group to group in rapidly changing and specialized circumstances. There are a great many leadership models that support learning how to do this. Here are three of the classics from the second half of the twentieth century:

1. **The task versus relationship model** requires leaders to balance the need to get the job done with an equally important need to build relationships.
2. **The autocrat-democrat-permissive model** features three leadership styles. It's based on research that shows that permissive and autocratic styles are far less productive than democratic styles.
3. **The Hay Group model** is more recent, from the 1990s. It reveals six styles: visionary, friendship, pacesetter, commanding, coaching and democratic. These six are also research-based and show a clear connection between making profit and leadership style. The two styles that are most profitable are visionary and friendship and the two least profitable are commanding and pacesetting. However, the authors recommend blending all the styles according to need.

BALANCE GETTING WORK DONE WITH BUILDING HEALTHY RELATIONSHIPS

Secret 28, *Be a team player*, describes the situational team-building model with its four stages of team formation. This is based on the idea that, at the start of a team experience, the emphasis should be on the task and ensuring that everyone has a clear idea of team goals, their individual responsibilities and what is needed to do their job. As soon as the task is under way, building strong relationships becomes more important, so that team members can support one another more effectively. It's the leader's job to balance getting the work done with encouraging good working relationships. This means adapting behaviour to meet changing circumstances.

Some leaders are more naturally task oriented while others are more people or relationship oriented. An Internet search produces hundreds of websites that offer free tests so that you can discover which orientation you have. The main benefit of this model is its simplicity: once learned, it's difficult to forget. It's also easy to apply.

If you focus on task at the start of a working relationship, you learn what your new colleague is like as a person as you carry on working together. This introduction shows the way to build a relationship. Later, if you notice that colleague's motivation slipping, you already have a connection and so can invite a conversation about how he or she is doing. Adaptive behaviour in this model is shifting from one orientation to the other as necessary and appropriate.

SAY YES, NO OR MAYBE IN THE RIGHT WAY AT THE RIGHT TIME

Another classic model features three kinds of behaviour: democratic, autocratic and permissive. It's based on research from the 1950s that compared productivity and social behaviour within groups that were led using one of these three styles. They found that a democratic style produced more and better work than an autocratic style and that a permissive style produced the least amount and poorest quality of work.

However, this tells only part of the story. Sometimes, as a leader, you have to say no, although your colleagues prefer a yes. This is autocratic behaviour, and is only harmful as a style if you never confer with your colleagues, never listen, and always insist that things be done your way. Saying no is entirely legitimate and necessary when you believe it's right and also when you have overall responsibility for results.

The permissive style is also necessary when working with highly creative and independent people. Likened to herding cats, these professionals need a leader with a light touch. Push or pull creative people and they simply ignore you. Listening to them (democratic) or saying 'No, you can't' (autocratic) is equally ignored. The idea is to allow them to get on with it until they produce what is needed, although this can be frustrating for leaders. The permissive style is also useful when leading a team that has worked together for a long time.

The democratic style is an all-weather perennial. You can never go wrong if you ask for opinions and listen respectfully. In fact, if this is how you normally behave, then everyone will co-operate fully when you need to act the autocrat.

CHOOSE FROM SIX STYLES

The 1990s study of leadership style by the Hay Group identified six styles and also saw which had a positive impact on profitability. Daniel Goleman, thought leader for emotional intelligence, reported these results and suggested that leaders should choose a style to suit each situation and blend the styles as necessary.

- **Visionary** – this style offers an inspiring vision that draws people together. It has the most positive impact on profit and is useful during times of turmoil and change.
- **Friendship** – this style builds strong bonds. It had the second most positive impact on profit and is useful when relationships need healing.
- **Commanding** – this style demands obedience without question. It has an overall negative impact on profit, but is useful in a crisis, bringing everyone together fast.
- **Pacesetting** – this style sets high standards and pushes people to perform. It has the second worst impact on profit because unnecessary errors are made when people are rushed and when listening drops to zero, but is useful for getting fast results from a motivated and expert team.

- **Democratic** – this style draws everyone into the discussion and works to create consensus. It has a positive impact on profit and is useful when equal partners need to work together and experts have valuable ideas to offer.
- **Coaching** – this style invests in people's development. It has a positive impact on profit and is useful for ensuring success in the long term.

Putting it all together

Modern leadership depends upon adaptability, and most – if not all – widely used leadership models recommend blending a variety of styles. This means changing your behaviour to meet the needs of each situation. Some people object to this because it feels false. They want to be the same person to everyone, although they already change their behaviour in their everyday life – when they move from sports to work to grocery shopping to taking the children to the park.

Adaptable leadership is a refinement of this ability to shift gears when changing from one activity to another. It acknowledges that a junior person on the team needs support and should be treated differently from a long-serving and independent member. In fact, veteran members of staff may resent being treated like 'newbies'. Pretending to be a different person is phoney. Changing behaviour to get results is professionalism.

44 DARE TO BE DIFFERENT

'The most courageous act is still to think for yourself. Aloud.'
Coco Chanel

'Whenever you find yourself on the side of the majority, it is time to pause and reflect.'
Mark Twain

'I believe that the most important single thing, beyond discipline and creativity, is daring to dare.'
Maya Angelou

'To be yourself in a world that is constantly trying to make you something else is the greatest accomplishment.'
Ralph Waldo Emerson

'Two roads diverged in a wood, and I –
I took the one less traveled by,
And that has made all the difference.'
Robert Frost

The Japanese have a saying: 'The tallest nail gets the hammer.' This means that it's best to avoid standing out in the crowd. The saying suggests that it's more important to blend into the group and be an anonymous member of the community. Even the achievement of excellence or the possession of physical beauty – features that set people apart – have value only as sources of inspiration for everyone to share. Individual pride is not really acceptable.

Daring to be different on purpose in that society is misguided and those who are different naturally suffer for it. Although Western society seemingly accepts diversity, under the surface there are similarities with Japan. Being a member of a minority in terms of race, age, sexuality or religion, or having a disability or health problem, sets a person apart and can cause real hardship.

Difference resulting from winning a prize or having special talent, charisma or enormous wealth is easier to accept in the West, but being different in any way is always an issue.

Whether positive or negative, in terms of society's judgement, difference creates outsiders, people who lack safety in numbers and who cannot settle quietly into the crowd. The expression 'lonely at the top' describes a situation where status, power and control are actually sources of loneliness. Although their success is attractive, these leaders are the ones who always stay late to finish a report, create unease when they arrive at a staff party, and stop conversation dead when they drop into the coffee room for a doughnut.

Daring to be different for these leaders isn't a choice – any more than it is for those at the margins of society or for those who have suffered failure or loss. Exclusion, isolation and loneliness go along with being different. It is lonely because different people are so often left alone. This is where the Japanese expression gives fair warning for the lack of popularity arising from saying and doing anything unusual.

It takes courage to decide to step out of line and risk being misunderstood. If the motive is self-expression or a righteous cause, it can be a satisfying experience.

DECIDE IF YOU WANT TO BE DIFFERENT

Stand in front of a full-length mirror, wearing casual clothes, and look at yourself – from the top of your head to your feet. Your task is to study the way you look and decide whether you want to be different in some way. You need to really look, as if you are seeing a different person. Have a pencil and paper ready to take a few notes.

These questions will help you get started. You can add others as well.

- Does anything surprise you about your appearance?
- Do you look taller or shorter than you imagine yourself to be?

- Are your shoulders held square or are they rounded?
- How is your weight distributed?
- If you want to lose or gain weight, how long has this been a good intention?
- Can you accept your weight as it is?
- Do you look tired?
- When your face is at rest, do you smile?
- What expression do you read in your own eyes?
- Do you like the way you look?
- Do you look different from people you know or do you think you blend in well?

You can use this activity as the start of a personal audit. You can also study other aspects of your personality, such as the way you respond to emotions and ideas. If you begin keeping a journal to record your reactions to decision making, problem solving or completing assignments, it will help you identify what makes you unique – that is, your blend of physical, emotional and mental strengths and weaknesses. This is your starting point for daring to be different.

CREATE NEW ROUTINES AND CHALLENGE OLD IDEAS

Changing any habit is difficult, but it is even harder if this is a mental habit or if you want to change your point of view. The certainties in life and known routines are so safe. This can stop anyone from changing, even when they are open to new possibilities in work and in life.

A way to get started is to question whether some of the 'shoulds' in your life are still relevant. For example, you may still have responsibility for work that's better delegated to a colleague in need of the experience. Try to catch yourself just as you automatically begin a task that is a routine. Ask yourself whether you really should do it and, if not, pass it on.

Next, consider whether there are projects that are more appropriate to your skills but a lack of time has kept you from starting them. These are your new 'shoulds', and you can find time if you delegate the work you've outgrown. Routine and habit can become a rigid and self-protecting shell that you carry everywhere you go. The result is difficulty when you want to start something new, assume a bigger challenge or just dare to be different.

HAVE A STORY, JOKE OR SONG

An Irish-American tradition from the last century required everyone attending a family or social occasion to prepare a short piece intended to entertain the rest of the gathering. A few days before the event, parents would ask their children, 'What have you got?' with the expectation that they were already preparing a story, joke or song, just in case they were asked to perform.

During the get-together, the host would ask, 'Has anyone got anything?' – knowing, of course, that there would a positive response. Someone would stand and share, then another and another. Each performance increased the feeling of togetherness and family unity. Regardless of quality, the applause would be heartfelt for the effort.

In a similar way, your job as a leader is to bring people together. Rather than entertain, however, your role is to provide a focus during meetings and other business gatherings. You'll add a great deal of value to that performance if, in advance, you ask yourself, 'What have I got?' It takes daring, if it's not your style, to tell a story or joke, but you'll be far more interesting and memorable if you do. A choice that relates to the meeting's content or to current business events would work best, but an unrelated offering can work equally well. It's your attitude of wanting to bring something extra that works.

Putting it all together

Daring to be different can put you at an extreme. The fringes of society can be at one extreme and the heroic centre of attention at the other, with awards, praise and photos on every magazine cover. Daring to be different also shows you have the courage to choose a difficult path. Given this level of challenge, it's best to be clear about what you want.

Leaders on occasion have to make tough choices that separate them from everyone else. Being brave can also be very lonely and so the reward needs to be worth having.

Attention seeking for its own sake intensifies isolation because people get tired of the performance. If it's linked to a cause, however – whether business or social – then eventually this brings a positive result.

Charity fun runs wearing unusual clothes, sponsored activities where leaders shave heads or faces, dye their hair or sleep rough overnight on the streets are examples of daring to be different that bring people together and raise awareness. Whatever the source of your difference, the key is choosing to use it wisely and well.

45 SHARE THE GLORY

*'A good leader takes a little more than a share of the blame,
a little less than a share of the credit.'*
Arnold H. Glasow

*'My grandfather once told me that there were two kinds of
people: those who do the work and those who take the credit.
He told me to try to be in the first group; there was much
less competition.'*
Indira Gandhi

*'It is amazing what you can accomplish if you do not care
who gets the credit.'*
Harry S. Truman

*'Great discoveries and improvements invariably involve
the co-operation of many minds. I may be given credit for
having blazed the trail, but when I look at the subsequent
developments I feel the credit is due to others rather
than to myself.'*
Alexander Graham Bell

'Soldiers generally win battles; generals get credit for them.'
Napoleon Bonaparte

In his quote above, Alexander Graham Bell recognizes the
importance of co-operation. Although he was, in his own words,
a trailblazer, he acknowledged the ideas, skills and efforts of
all those who went before him and those who would take his
discoveries forward. His modesty is attractive and enhances his
achievements. It also has the ring of truth to it, as if he truly
wants to give credit where it's due.

Saying 'thank you' to teammates and colleagues for working
together successfully is a gracious gesture that invites good

feeling. Leaders who also give fair credit to those who actually do the work gain everyone's trust and respect. Their show of honest dealing often leads to their receiving opportunities that are denied those who claim all the credit for themselves. Such self-promoters may also suffer reputation damage and find themselves excluded from honours later that they may actually deserve.

In the 1960s Jocelyn Bell, as she was then named, was studying astrophysics at Cambridge University when she discovered pulsars, or pulsating stars. However, credit for this was given to her supervisor Anthony Hewish, although, when she first showed him her data, he assured her that it was nothing but man-made interference. Only when she had proved beyond doubt that her findings were genuine did Hewish agree.

Later, when her discovery led to Hewish winning the Nobel Prize in Physics in 1974, the scientific community went into an uproar of protest and nicknamed the physics award that year the 'No-Bell Prize'. Hewish, of course, had the option of at least asking the Nobel Committee to consider including Bell, but he chose not to do this. Jocelyn was gracious, saying that it was normal for teachers to be recognized for a student's work, in the same way they are held to blame for a student's mistakes.

Hewish's prize, when mentioned in the years that followed, always came with the rider that he'd failed to give proper credit to Bell. It didn't matter that the later named Dame Jocelyn Bell Burnell said she was happy with the Nobel Committee's decision. The world felt differently and never let Hewish forget it. Dame Bell Burnell went on to receive coveted awards, distinctions and honours of every kind, while prize committees largely ignored Hewish after 1974. He continued his scientific research, but he must have felt the quiet reproach.

SHARE THE CREDIT AS A HABIT

Hewish is an extreme example. It's rare that excluding a colleague from getting credit for their work gets such wide notice or is so harshly criticized, but it is a risk. It is better to avoid this entirely and share credit scrupulously.

As a leader, you set the tone. Make sure that any rivalry is healthy, with clear guidance about who gets what reward and for which work. You can use scoring in sport as a guide for giving credit. Both goals and the assistance given to win the goal are usually counted. At work, final achievements as well as supporting roles can be given credit as well. Make it clear what 'assisting' means so that it shows the way to success.

If you have someone on the team who wants more than his or her fair share, then this needs careful management. Too often, the squeaky wheel gets the oil. Colleagues who constantly ask for special assignments, promotion, salary increases or time off tend to get them just because they are so annoying. They never stop whining and have no shame about demanding more than their due.

Giving in to this kind of person too often demoralizes everyone else. It helps if you have a system in place that assures everyone that objective measures are used for any rewards or special treatment. This won't stop the nagging, but it supports saying no when necessary.

KNOW WHAT PEOPLE ARE DOING

Having a regular discussion, either one to one or in a group, about what everyone is doing helps clarify where credit is due. One idea is a meeting at the start of the week where everyone gives a short description of what they hope to achieve. Then, at the end of the week, have another short meeting with a recap of goals and a summary of what was actually achieved. This end-of-week meeting also gives people an opportunity to discuss distractions and explain their need for any additional support.

This is valuable information for a leader. If you also ask everyone to store the weekly goals and achievements in a shared folder online, this provides a basis for employee performance reviews. The accumulation of achievements is also a motivation booster as, week by week, progress is made to achieve goals. Further, it's easier to see who is doing more and better work when it's time for promotion.

You can also see who may be stuck doing the jobs no one else wants and who is carrying more than their fair share. Burnout is the inevitable result of an unevenly shared workload. However, it takes skilled leadership to create balance. The first step is getting at least a month's worth of information about who is doing what. Then you can think about identifying who should accept more challenge and who should share more routine work.

GIVE YOURSELF CREDIT AS WELL

This secret so far has been about making sure that other people are fairly acknowledged. This assumes that people will know what part you played and give you the credit you deserve. This may not always be the case and, if you are the kind of person who feels uncomfortable when praised, you may want to avoid situations where this may happen. The result could be that you don't receive your due.

An extremely modest leader can be a problem, for two reasons:

1. Not taking credit can mean that those who work with and for you may not get praise and approval either. This can lower morale and risk holding people back.
2. If you haven't taken credit for your body of work, you will be unlikely to be given interesting opportunities in future.

There are several remedies for this. A way to take credit without feeling as if you are boasting is to praise the work of your team. However, you need also to describe the role you played. Using an objective style, simply present what each person achieved. Describe the part you, as leader, played using verbs like initiated, analysed, directed, envisioned and managed – that is, any verb that describes taking full responsibility.

Receiving your fair share of recognition for a job well done means that sooner or later you will be asked to progress to even more interesting and exciting work.

Putting it all together

Leaders need to share the glory. Pushing to the front to claim credit for work other people have done creates a bad feeling that never goes away. In fact, this behaviour gives good cause to colleagues to look elsewhere for a leader. But leaders who willingly share the glory seem to get more of it, as well as praise for being generous.

Dame Bell Burnell has been a major force in science throughout her life and she has encouraged, through her teaching and research, many young people to go on to do great things as well. She said, 'I have discovered that even if you do describe it as an injustice you can do incredibly well out of not getting a Nobel Prize.' She offers a lesson in being gracious. If you are ever ignored for your achievements, accept this with dignity and continue to build, create and prosper without bitterness or regret.

46 MAKE FRIENDS AND FORM ALLIANCES

'Confront issues and challenges – not each other.'
Suzanne Mayo Frindt

*'Leadership has a harder job to do than just choose sides.
It must bring sides together.'*
Jesse Jackson

*'If you need something from somebody, always give that
person a way to hand it to you.'*
Sue Monk Kidd

'Be nice to geeks; you'll probably end up working for one.'
Bill Gates

*'With some people you spend an evening: with
others you invest it.'*
Colin Powell

Co-operative people are often more successful than those who
are self-serving. They form alliances that create mutual benefit
they wouldn't receive if working alone. They also know the value
of giving tips and sharing information freely because their friends
and allies do the same for them. By contrast, people who like to
stand alone lack a helping hand to pull them up when they fall
down, as inevitably everyone does.

Thirty years ago Robert Axelrod researched how civilization
could possibly have developed in a world filled with cut-throats
and self-interested people. He also wondered how human beings
have survived as a species, given the compulsion to win at all
costs, do violence, sneak, cheat and lie. Logically, this survival
didn't make any sense to him. His answer was alliances.

He discovered through a computer tournament (see Secret 37, *Give people a second chance*) that people make friends and form alliances as a means of self-preservation. They identify potential allies, agree to watch one another's back, and create safety in numbers. They keep their agreements and together they create and share prosperity. Axelrod also suggested that the present casts a shadow over the future. Allies know this and realize that behaving badly in the present could cost them support in future. However, if they pick the wrong ally, they can end up worse off than if they were alone. It also matters how their alliances are formed.

Here is a checklist as a starting point for choosing the right allies:

1. Partner with smart people, with 'smart' meaning that they understand that cheating hurts everyone, not just the one being cheated. ☐
2. Be absolutely clear what the partnership means. Ambiguity causes confusion, disruption and misunderstanding and is avoided by clear guidance at the start. ☐
3. Decide in advance how to unwind the alliance amicably when or if circumstances change for one of the parties. ☐
4. Be forgiving and seek an explanation for seeming misdeeds. Your allies may assume their motives are clear. ☐
5. If there is just cause, however, withdraw support until or unless they say sorry. (See Secret 37, *Give people a second chance*.) ☐

AVOID CONFRONTATION

Tom O' Daly is the recently appointed team leader to a group of 20 engineers. When he accepted the job, his new boss warned him that one of his new colleagues had wanted the job badly. So when he arrives to work on his first day, he's not all that surprised to see that the open-plan office he visited the week before is rearranged.

Twenty desks formerly spaced in clusters around the room in line with specialist areas are now tightly positioned in rows, with his own desk moved to the far end of the room and separated from the others by a bank of filing cabinets. No one looks up as the lift doors open and Tom steps into the room. Seeing the situation at a glance, he knows his next step is important and crucial to creating good relationships with his new team.

Ignoring the desk arrangement, Tom heads for the nearest engineer and introduces himself. The engineer is surprised, looks up and accepts Tom's extended hand. As Tom asks intelligent questions about his work and listens to the answers, so does everyone else. After a few minutes, Tom then moves to the engineer next in the row.

By his fourth introduction, it's obvious he plans to meet and greet everyone in the room. In the process, he's revealed an impressive understanding of the problems the team has to address through comments he makes to each engineer.

BE GENEROUS AND ACCEPT OTHER PEOPLE'S FADS AND FOIBLES

By the tenth engineer, everyone is openly listening to the conversations. By the 15th, the banter begins as they all add details to the others' introductions: of both successes and humorous accounts of failures. When one calls out to another, 'Tell him about when it all went pear-shaped!' Tom laughs and the atmosphere becomes far more relaxed.

When he's finally met everyone in the room, Tom walks back to the lift, looks around and quietly asks, 'Where's my desk?' There's a silence and then suddenly everyone laughs, although a few with less enthusiasm. Then the two engineers nearest the filing cabinets move Tom's desk to its original position, carefully aligning the legs to their old carpet indentations.

Tom's behaviour is well judged. He avoids confrontation by ignoring the team's hostility and setting his own agenda. Rather than making an issue of desks and office space, he sets about making friends. This takes confidence and the belief that he can turn things around. Then, when his introductions begin to break the ice, he carries on without commenting that he'd like to win them over.

An angry or frustrated reaction would have made him look like a cry baby. And he would be one, if he had reacted to such a childish power play from his new colleagues. He knows that leadership is tough and that most of the time people won't like him. Even when he's in the right, he knows that at times it's more important to be smart, make friends of potential enemies and win people over to his side.

EXPAND YOUR INFLUENCE

Tom created allies among his colleagues one by one. This method will also work when you want to increase your influence and gain greater recognition as an expert in your field. Everyone you meet can potentially introduce you to others that you can meet as well, one by one. The first step is to decide what kind of network you want and what function you need it to perform.

For example, you may want to get a better job. To achieve this with networking, you should begin by listing everyone you know who has the kind of job you want. If you don't know anyone directly in that job, then identify someone to introduce you to someone else who knows someone. Even if you start with no leads at all, when you persevere, gradually you'll gain new contacts of the kind you need. Someone will always be helpful. Someone will eventually give you the information you want.

There's a science behind building a social network. A few years ago, engineers at Microsoft decided to see how closely their email customers were connected to one another. They looked at 3 billion messages and found, with few exceptions, that everyone was truly part of a huge network, separated by an average of just 6.5 connections. So no matter how far you imagine you are from meeting the people you want to meet, with determination and a systematic approach you can make it happen.

Putting it all together

Friends and allies are there to support you in difficult times, just as you are there for them. Mutual aid and co-operation are the basis of civilization and they ensure that laws are obeyed and that the community is safe. It's a challenge, however, to find the right allies. This can also feel like manipulation and using people, but this isn't the case. There's a different spirit driving your search for allies for a professional purpose. In this case, you want to help other people as much as you hope they will support you.

In the computer tournament, those who played a solitary and self-serving game simply lost (see Secret 37). The winning games all co-operated. However, it takes skill to find shared solutions where everyone wins. It also can seem far easier and time saving to get on with things alone. This is true until you want to achieve a challenging goal: this takes a united effort where everyone gains. It's well worth this effort because self-defence takes resources of time and energy. When like-minded people share and everyone works together for a common good, then resources are free for other uses.

47 BE LUCKY

'The best luck of all is the luck you make for yourself.'
Douglas MacArthur

'It's a funny thing: the more I practise, the luckier I get.'
Jack Nicklaus

'Luck is not chance, it's toil; fortune's expensive smile is earned.'
Emily Dickinson

'Luck is believing you're lucky.'
Tennessee Williams

'I believe life is a series of near misses. A lot of what we ascribe to luck is not luck at all. It's seizing the day and accepting responsibility for your future.'
Howard Schultz

Lucky people have confidence. They smile at the right time to the right people, who then smile at them in return. Doors open and they pass through, happy to accept whatever is offered. When damaged by events, they bounce back. Even when held down for a long time, they win through and smile again. They are just plain lucky.

Or are they? There are people who don't believe in luck as a mystical force that decides that some people win and others lose. They argue that winning is a matter of probability and a statistical event. Someone has to win and there is nothing special about those who do. These pragmatists would argue the truly lucky person is the one who is smart enough to have a positive attitude and face challenges with a smile.

This secret agrees with this and, further, that luck isn't about winning a prize, a good job, birth into a wealthy family, physical beauty or something else. 'Luck' is an attitude that becomes a magnet for good things, people and events. Smiling isn't the result of luck. It comes from within, but it can create very lucky and positive results. After all, saying hello in a friendly way to everyone eventually leads to greeting the right person.

However, carrying the lucky label is a big benefit. Napoleon once asked, when given the name of a general to lead a charge, 'I know he's a good general, but is he lucky?' He wanted generals who believe in their own luck and have the associated confidence to drive a charge. When faced with terrible odds, they would assume that their luck would hold. This would force them to find an opportunity that an ordinary – or *unlucky* – person would never imagine could exist.

Here are examples of both lucky and unlucky people:

- Two photographers go into the woods. One moves quietly, looks for signs that game passed that way, finds a trail, waits and watches in silence with camera ready, then snaps the perfect shot. The other wears heavy shoes, ignores the trail, gets thirsty and drinks just as the game passes, and so misses the shot.
- Two players end practice the evening before a big match. One eats a balanced meal following the coach's advice, goes to bed and rises early the next morning, has a good breakfast, goes to the field feeling relaxed and rested, and scores a fantastic goal. The other goes stright to the bar, gets drunk, eats a greasy burger and chips, falls asleep after midnight, gets to the field at the last minute, and then misses every play.

CREATE YOUR OWN LUCK

The successful photographer and player put preparation into getting lucky. Poor players, incompetent photographers and everyone else can improve their luck dramatically with discipline and hard work. Changing behaviour improves the odds of a successful outcome and therefore leads to better luck. But what kind of behaviour creates a better result?

The media is full of stories about supposedly lucky people. On a closer look, however, we realize that many of them have made their own luck. Make a list of lucky people you admire and think of them in different situations. Identify how they behave when they:

- are criticized or receive praise
- win or lose
- are surrounded by powerful people or by vulnerable ones
- are given advice by an expert
- spend time with family and friends.

Think about how they walk, stand, smile, hold their head, gesture with their hands, listen and speak. Think about the kinds of things they say. Now consider which behaviour most expresses confidence, self-belief, or ease with life. Choose one example of behaviour to copy. Make it something that suits your personality, gender, age or appearance.

After you choose, imagine yourself behaving like the lucky person. Mentally put yourself in everyday situations acting like the lucky person. Listen, speak and smile the way that person would. Identify the differences between how you act and how the lucky person acts. Ask yourself how you can change to behave more like that person.

ACT AS IF YOU ARE LUCKY

Some psychologists say that you can change the way you feel by changing the way you act. For example, the act of smiling – stretching your lips and raising your cheek muscles – can actually alter your mood. In other words, smiling can lead to feelings of happiness in the same way that happy feelings can make you smile.

Muhammad Ali said, 'To be a great champion you must believe you are the best. If you're not, pretend you are.' This applies to being lucky as well. If you act as if you are lucky, then other people will react towards you as if you are truly lucky. This in turn creates a virtuous circle, with their belief in you amplifying your self-belief.

But what exactly do you think is lucky? Is it winning a prize, getting a great job or spending time with people you love? Your beliefs about luck are linked to what you value. To discover more about your values, ask yourself what in your life would you most regret losing. For many people this is family or friends. For some it's a valuable item, a house, a car or treasured photographs. Knowing what you want to keep shows what is most important to you. It shows what you believe you need in order to be and feel lucky.

LEARN FROM LUCKY PEOPLE

In times of adversity and misfortune, the way you react often dictates what happens to you next. Lucky people have the knack of bouncing back from loss, failure or painful illness. Even if they suffer for an extended period, they recover from the decline. It takes a positive mental attitude to turn around a bad situation and avoid sinking into self-pity and regret.

You can learn from lucky people so that you react in a more positive way, even when you feel your worst. To do this, think of the last time you failed at something that was really important to you. Remember the details – physically, emotionally and mentally – at the moment you realized you had failed. If you felt sick, upset or anxious, remember it. Put yourself in that situation, even if you dislike remembering it.

Now think of a lucky person and consider how he or she would react in a similar situation. Imagine that the lucky person is with you and reacting to your recent failure alongside you. How does he or she behave? Is there anything about that behaviour that you could copy next time so that your reactions are more alike? The goal is for you to get to a point where you say to yourself, whatever happens, 'I'm so lucky that everything works for me.'

Putting it all together

It's surprisingly controversial to suggest that people make their own luck. People who believe that things just happen to them without warning, or that their lives are out of their control, see luck as another force that dominates their actions. Others dismiss this view. They assume that they shape their own lives with personal choice and want to believe that they are responsible for whatever happens to them.

Luck as an external source of good things and surprising rewards can continue to be debated by these two groups, but there's no question that positive results arise from a positive attitude and hard work. The 'lucky' shot played by a top golfer happens after thousands of hours of practice and their learning how to read the wind, the air and the terrain. Winning the game isn't the result of an unseen and magical intervention.

Hard work and being alert to opportunity so often lead to a happy outcome. Call it lucky or something else, but it is the mainstay of good leaders everywhere. Then, just in case there is a magical force, you will be even better off if all your hard work is multiplied by luck if it does decide to strike you after all.

48 RELAX AND HAVE FUN

'Every now and then go away, have a little relaxation, for when you come back to your work your judgement will be surer. Go some distance away because then the work appears smaller and more of it can be taken in at a glance and a lack of harmony and proportion is more readily seen.'

Leonardo da Vinci

'One can discover more about a person in an hour of play than in a year of conversation.'

Plato

'The more you praise and celebrate your life, the more there is in life to celebrate.'

Oprah Winfrey

'What most people don't understand is that UFOs are on a cosmic tourist route. That's why they're always seen in Arizona, Scotland and New Mexico. Another thing to consider is that all three of those destinations are good places to play golf. So there's possibly some connection between aliens and golf.'

Alice Cooper

'It is requisite for the relaxation of the mind that we make use, from time to time, of playful deeds and jokes.'

St Thomas Aquinas

One definition of relaxation is 'rest from work or engaging in an enjoyable activity in order to become less tired or anxious'. This means a time-out period to recharge and be generally idle – on purpose – in order to be ready for more work. Too much relaxation makes a person lazy, but too much work leads to stress-related illness. Very busy leaders can fall under the spell of working too much and forgetting that they need to stop, rest and relax at regular intervals.

Recreation is the chance to withdraw from work and have a rethink. Distance from work allows the development of a different perspective so that even the most challenging problems can seem less so after a time-out to relax. However, there are people who say with a straight face that work is their idea of fun and relaxation. It may certainly be true that they enjoy, like or even love their work, but by definition work is not fun and it is certainly not relaxation.

Work is focused activity to achieve goals. Fun is pure enjoyment with the purpose of creating laughter, smiles and relaxation. It enables the body to use different muscle groups and the mind to focus on taste, sound, sight, scent and touch. The five senses are the basis of simple pleasure. Serving these senses leads to a healthy digestion, a relaxed body, creative thoughts, a positive and even sunny mood, and a good night's sleep.

Enjoyment is necessary for a balanced life. And anyone who says they don't need this has forgotten what it feels like to run on the beach, watch silly movies with friends, play sport as if survival depended on winning a round of drinks, or rest on green grass in a gentle breeze. Add family and friends to the mix and this produces a 'smoothie of happy'.

Leadership requires long hours, can be highly stressful, and places demands on every aspect of a person's life. This can make finding time for fun a worthy challenge, so a real time-saver is to laugh at work. From time to time, create situations where everyone laughs together in a stress-free environment. A positive mental attitude leads to greater intake of oxygen and healthy blood flow. Even the most stressful work can then happen in a calm and happy workplace.

RELAX YOUR MUSCLES

This technique trains your body to relax fully by tensing groups of muscles and suddenly relaxing them as you move your attention from your feet to the top of your head. It takes about 15 minutes and should be done daily for at least a month. The longer you train, on a regular basis, the easier it becomes to relax your whole body quickly just by thinking of it. This enables you to relax fully when facing stressful situations, including public speaking, hearing bad news and working long hours.

This technique is among the easiest of the eyes-closed activities because there's something physical to focus on throughout. Although falling asleep can be a problem for some people at first, with practice it becomes easier to stay alert and complete the exercise. First find a quiet place where you won't be interrupted for the whole 15 minutes and then turn your phone off.

Sit on a straight-backed chair to help stay awake. Breathe in to the count of three and out to the same count. Do this several times until it feels easy to do so. Then focus on your right foot and tighten your foot muscles to the count of three as you breathe in. Hold the tension to the count of five and then suddenly release both your breath and muscles so that you are fully relaxed. Count to ten slowly, breathing gently.

Repeat this process, tensing and relaxing groups of muscles in the sequence listed here: right foot, right calf, right thigh, left foot, left calf, left thigh, buttocks, abdomen, chest, right hand, right forearm, right upper arm, left hand, left forearm, left upper arm, upper torso, neck and shoulders, face and scalp. Working the scalp takes practice but it is possible.

SLOW DOWN

Rushing around while living a highly pressured life gets in the way of having fun and relaxing. Here is a list of things you can do to help you slow down:

- Stretch and yawn loudly whenever you catch yourself crouching over your desk.
- Sing out loud and choose songs that make you feel happy when doing small jobs.
- Listen to people without nodding your head or moving facial muscles – just listen.
- Treat everyone to ice cream and watch them eat it; then, after they're finished, treat yourself.

- Jump in your car and drive nowhere special while listening to music.
- Cook yourself a meal of all your favourite foods; eat slowly, tasting every bite.
- Make sounds of enjoyment as you eat – you may have to do this alone.
- Watch the kind of comedy film where people fall over and the jokes are really stupid.
- Laugh at least once each day, so hard that you cry.
- Sit or walk around outdoors every day with no other purpose than being outdoors.
- Train yourself to turn off worrying thoughts so that you fully stop your brain.
- Smile and nod at someone you see every day but do not know.
- Take the stairs rather than the lift for at least four floors.
- Instead of queuing to buy coffee, stand outside watching people and traffic go by.
- Remove one activity from your daily routine; don't replace it; and then do everything else more slowly.
- Think of at least three more ideas for slowing down.

CHOOSE YOUR ATTITUDE

Mental habits take hold and don't easily let go. If they're positive and wholesome, this is a good thing. If they're driven by worry and stress, they can be damaging. Time pressure, responsibility and the serious nature of earning a living and making money often lead to a whole day at work without smiling even once. This is a problem because it signals a lack of relaxation.

The day may start well, with a good morning for everyone, but as situations arise and events progress, stress can take hold. Only your attitude can control your reactions and ensure that you maintain balance all day long. Take a short time-out at intervals throughout the day to evaluate your attitude. Smile when you say thanks for a report. Look out of the window or walk slowly around your workplace. Ask yourself why you're rushing if you notice you're being brusque with colleagues.

Find something pleasing to look at and make yourself – even if it feels forced – be grateful for what you have. These are mental health breaks, and they work so that you can say good night to everyone in as friendly a manner as you said good morning.

Putting it all together

Relaxing and having fun are essential for all aspects of health: mental, emotional and physical. Relaxation is an antidote to tension and better than medication for preventing stress-related symptoms. Laughter, play and enjoyment allow you to get away from thinking about work and help you gain perspective. Having a hobby, sport or other recreation in your life ensures that you keep work and life in balance.

Relaxation balances tension of every kind, and together they create a cycle of rest and activity. This works well as long as the shift from one to the other is made consciously, so that regular breaks paced at healthy intervals are normal. This approach provides lifelong protection against stress-related illness and ensures a good quality of life along with happy relationships.

49 HAVE A BIG IDEA

'High sentiments always win in the end. The leaders who offer blood, toil, tears and sweat always get more out of their followers than those who offer safety and a good time. When it comes to the pinch, human beings are heroic.'
George Orwell

'Go as far as you can see; when you get there, you'll be able to see farther.'
J. P. Morgan

'The only thing worse than being blind is having sight but no vision.'
Helen Keller

'Be daring, be different, be impractical, be anything that will assert integrity of purpose and imaginative vision against the play-it-safers, the creatures of the commonplace, the slaves of the ordinary.'
Cecil Beaton

'Don't let negativity affect your vision. A lot of people have said harsh things, but I don't let it affect me. If anything, it gives me more enthusiasm and pushes me to do better in my career so I can prove them wrong.'
Nicole Polizzi

Having a big idea means looking to the horizon for possibility and opportunity, rather than looking to see whether the lights are still on at the late-night service station – the one next to the supermarket and dry cleaners. These places may well be there on a distant hill, but a leader in the process of developing a big idea doesn't think about them. Managers think about filling the tank with petrol. Leaders look to the distance to discover a big idea.

In marketing, a big idea refers to improving or transforming a brand. In government, it describes a major initiative or push for change. In leadership, it means looking at a situation, seeing all its parts and examining how they fit together, and then discovering alternative ways to make them work. This can create a new situation entirely or transform an old one to be fit for a new and bigger purpose. Either way, a big idea propels a leader forward to explore new ground and accept a bigger challenge.

Big ideas provide an ideal for everyone to pursue together, but should also be practical enough to plan how to achieve them. Big ideas inspire people to take action. Most leading universities offer a 'big idea' competition. Their purpose is to present their institutions as cutting edge. Major technology companies do the same, but in their case they want to identify talented people in order to recruit them. Having a big idea is a positive signal that says 'I have vision'. In fast-changing environments, this is a necessity.

Leaders need a big idea because it keeps them competitive – not just their business or organization but themselves as employable people. The top is a desirable place to be and there are always people below scrambling for position. A great way to get someone else's spot is to offer a newer, better and bigger idea. Entrepreneurs know this well. The new business that gets financing is the one that inspires a 'Wow!' response.

However, pushing big ideas to the surface or forcing them to flower like hothouse blooms may be missing the point and the ideas can suffer in the process. The following strategy describes a better way.

ZONE OUT ON PURPOSE: EXPERIENCE *EUREKA!*

Zoning out is a chance for your mind to roam freely. Called daydreaming by parents and teachers, as in 'Stop your daydreaming!' it's a time when focused thinking stops and the brain takes a rest. Some people stare into space; others doodle on a page or gaze around without really taking in their surroundings.

But neuroscience research now shows that zoning out is both a highly productive and useful activity. Similar to computer downtime, scientists have found that taking a rest from thinking allows the brain to make new connections called synapses, which link ideas and allow new conclusions to be drawn. As you zone out, your brain is in overdrive, working in the background processing information and integrating previous experience.

Background processing creates those moments of sudden awareness or insight when solutions to complex problems seem to appear from nowhere. This can happen while making a sandwich, walking the dog or having a bath. The famous story of Archimedes, the third-century-BC Greek mathematician, illustrates this: he discovered that water displacement could be used to measure weight when his tub overflowed as he sank into it. He is reported to have called out 'Eureka!' – ancient Greek for 'I found it!'

You can create eureka moments on purpose by putting aside time to zone out. This is the reason why technology companies like Google give their engineers time to work on anything they wish for a certain number of hours per week. However, anyone can use the train or bus commute to work as zone-out, creativity time.

BE ORIGINAL

Lady Gaga, the mischievous and talented rock star with the interesting looks and outfits, says, 'I am a walking piece of art every day, with my dreams and my ambitions forward at all times in an effort to inspire my fans to lead their life in that way.' She's made herself her very own walking-and-talking big idea, and is a good role model for leaders who need to get their people to stretch out of their comfort zones.

This doesn't mean wearing a chicken suit to work. It does mean encouraging bold ideas by listening to your colleagues describe them. Instead of saying no and explaining why an idea won't work, you ask for some eureka time so that you can consider the idea's positive aspects. Even if the ideas are poor, listening to even the weaker ones will encourage future and more helpful suggestions.

Leaders who make a habit of having big ideas are always ready to hear if someone else has one on the boil. They make remarks like:

- 'Walk me through it.'
- 'What makes it new?'
- 'What are the parts?'
- 'Do they fit together in some other way as well?'

This last question is a big thinker's favourite and it signals that the idea is about to be hijacked for development in a new way.

AVOID TINY THINKING

In 2002 the leaders at General Motors set the company a target of capturing a 29 per cent market share in automotive sales by the end of the next financial year. This would mark an improvement from 28.6 per cent, their previous best number. Senior executives wore lapel pins with '29' on them to indicate that every decision had to be be guided by the drive to achieve that number.

There was huge investment in marketing and advertising as well as in a negative pricing campaign where every car sold was given an incentive discount of more than $3,200 (£2,100). Profitability was forgotten, as well as the need to compete with global car manufacturers who were innovating with technology and offering better customer service. Despite these efforts in 2003, GM didn't make its 29 per cent target, with one pundit saying that customers didn't care about GM's market share; they wanted to drive great cars with excellent service.

In 2005 the company posted a loss of $10.6 billion and in 2009 filed for bankruptcy. Its legacy of pension and health-care costs created crippling expenses at a time when its car sales bottomed. The company's main source of income came from its finance division, but even this couldn't balance the books. Every car produced cost more money to make and sell than it created income.

Whenever top people in an organization are preoccupied with a single number for a single aspect of the business, this is a tiny idea – not a big one. It doesn't matter where the CEO earned his or her MBA, or if the whole executive team is a band of high-earning professors. They are proposing a very tiny idea – not a big one. Of course, this observation has the benefit of hindsight, and is not intended to be a judgement. It is a tip so that others don't do the same.

Putting it all together

A big idea inspires and pulls people together. If the idea is then communicated effectively, it becomes more likely that it will succeed. Big ideas can appear from nowhere and smart leaders are on the watch for them. This is where social skills are helpful. They include listening carefully to discover a big idea from any source. Sometimes lack of experience gives a younger person an opportunity to see gaps or identify new solutions that people who are more familiar with the problem cannot see.

As a leader, you can also get new ideas by zoning out on purpose. Set aside time on a regular basis to allow your brain to process information in the background. This happens while you think random thoughts or idly turn over events in your mind. You may be thinking about remarks your colleagues made earlier, or making a shopping list, or glancing at bits of paper on your desk. Then without warning, there it is: the solution you need. Eureka!

50 MAKE PEOPLE YOUR MAIN BUSINESS

'Never look down on people unless you're helping them up.'
Jesse Jackson

'A desk is a dangerous place from which to view the world.'
John Le Carré

'I know of no single formula for success. But over the years
I have observed that some attributes of leadership are
universal and are often about finding ways of encouraging
people to combine their efforts, their talents, their insights,
their enthusiasm and their inspiration to work together.'
Queen Elizabeth II

'Outstanding leaders go out of their way to boost the
self-esteem of their personnel. If people believe in themselves,
it's amazing what they can accomplish.'
Sam Walton

'You cannot be a leader, and ask other people to follow you,
unless you know how to follow, too.'
Sam Rayburn

This book's introduction promised tips for improving leadership
skills and throughout there's been a single underlying message:
that leaders achieve results by working through other people.
This means valuing and respecting colleagues and empowering
them to act. Whether making decisions, planning business
growth, managing fear or taking risks, as well as a range of other
leadership activities, a leader's main business is people. Forget
this and leadership becomes a constant struggle.

People include peers, customers, family, rivals from other companies, enemies and friends. Identifying who key people are and what they want must be the central issue for everyone in charge. This is because leaders lead people – not firms, businesses or public bodies. Organizations and industries are not alive. They are merely ideas and ways to bring collections of people together to work towards and achieve goals. Getting things done requires remembering that people do this work.

Highly educated people with many years of experience can forget this on occasion and make less effective decisions as a result. These include an international financial services meltdown, a global food contamination scandal or a product recall of faulty goods that bankrupts a business.

Leaders can leave their brains at the door when they become overly fixed on a single growth idea, while forgetting that people both make and buy what that growth produces.

Staying focused on people and what they value is the source of robust and sustainable growth. It was ever thus. Pre-digital communication, and even pre-telegraph and pony express, made smart leaders act for and react to people rather than abstractions like 'economic reality', the 'bottom line' or 'increasing market share'. Several of this book's secrets suggest joining and actively participating in social and professional networks. This idea leads to contacts that can offer helpful advice and information.

When leaders put their people at the centre of their decision-making, this means they take a step back in terms of taking action themselves. Leaders who have felt valued for getting things done may need to make the transition from getting their own hands dirty to making things happen through others. This can be an unwelcome change at first, until they realize that their role is now bigger. Once they reach the top, they encourage other people to get things done while their job becomes envisioning the future.

CHOOSE TO BE LIKED

Psychologists at Harvard University suggest that people's minds wander about 47 per cent of the time and that while this is going on they don't pay attention to what they are actually doing. In Secret 49, *Have a big idea,* this is called 'zoning out' and is considered a good thing. In this secret it's more of a warning because information you believe you pass on to your colleagues may not actually be retrievable by them later.

When they blank you, it's not that they have forgotten; it's more that they never heard what you said in the first place. One option is to be prepared to repeat everything you say. Another idea comes from a different group of psychologists who suggest that you can capture people's attention with animated behaviour. This gets an emotional reaction and their intellectual attention soon follows this.

Smiling, using people's names, asking for their opinions and listening attentively are all ways to get an emotional response. It's like waking people up so that they pay attention to the other things you're saying as well. They will not only remember the encounter, but also all of what you said.

Dale Carnegie's influential book *How to Win Friends and Influence People,* first published in 1936, contains similar advice. This was one of the first self-improvement books to be written and it has sold 15 million copies worldwide. One of its guiding principles, and a slogan that Dale Carnegie used, is 'Don't criticize, condemn, or complain.' This is a positive way to behave that anyone can copy. It also supports creating a positive emotional reaction when you meet people and want them to listen to you.

ACCEPT BEING DISLIKED

Bringing unpleasant news, asking people to do things they dislike, denying requests for extra support and discussing performance failure are among many challenging tasks that can cause people to dislike you. These are the same people you need to *work through* in order to achieve goals and get work completed. Giving cause for people to dislike you – the very ones you need – is like squaring a circle.

There's an added problem for women as leaders. Research shows that women are expected to be kind and supportive at work as well as at home. This is such a strong stereotype – and so little questioned by even thinking men and women – that when work requires women to say no, they are disliked even more than men. This is unfortunate but, over time, women as leaders will become normal and their saying no will be more readily accepted as well. It's a process that requires patience, with younger leaders increasingly unaware that there was ever an issue. 'The wheels of change grind slow but exceedingly fine.'

More to the point, how can both men and women bosses be accepted – never mind liked – when they have to do things people dislike? The solution is to start by gaining trust and developing mutual respect. Create good connections with your colleagues so that, when you have to say no, you have a positive history. If you've been supportive often enough in the past, you'll get a free pass. This won't be from everyone, of course. There'll always be people who resent you no matter what you do.

Think of Tom O' Daly in Secret 46, *Make friends and form alliances*. He faced collective opposition on his first day of work, but used listening skills to connect with his new team. A few were reluctant, but the majority came round. This is normal. Work on building relationships one by one, person by person. Accept being disliked. As long as you also listen and give people a chance to grow and develop, you'll win through.

KNOW AND RESPECT YOUR STAKEHOLDERS

In the same way that you need to work through other people, your stakeholders often want to work through you. It's another of life's two-way streets, where co-operation and mutual support create win–win situations (see Secret 37, *Give people a second chance*). But first you need to know who your stakeholders are.

A definition of stakeholder is 'a person, group, or collection of groups that have a compelling interest in an activity, project or organization'.

Obvious examples are customers, suppliers, creditors, business directors, employees, owners or shareholders, unions and the surrounding community. Stakeholders by definition are affected by the actions taken by their stakeholding organization. They have a stake in it, after all. However, they don't always have any control or influence over actions. This can be a problem if they also lack a channel to voice concerns or offer suggestions.

Leaders who work well with stakeholders strengthen their connections with them and can gain their support. Stakeholders, singly and as a body, are potential allies. It's a useful exercise to identify them, make regular contact, and anticipate any need they may have for information in advance of their having to ask for this. A way to show respect is to acknowledge their need to know.

Not all stakeholders are obvious. Some committees and boards may meet only once a year but in that one session can decide the funding and fate of an organization. Identifying the individual members of a stakeholder group is crucial. Here's a checklist to help:

1. Go through old emails. If messages are archived regularly, go back a year and look for any names you've forgotten about. Start a list. ☐
2. Ask colleagues to think of the three most important people or groups that most affect your area's existence. Add them to the list. ☐
3. Ask your boss who is most important to him or her in terms of having to report about quality, productivity or future growth. Add any names to the list. ☐
4. Look at last year's reports to find names of signatories as well as groups that have played a part in the organization's success during the previous year. This will reveal key clients, suppliers and supervising groups. Add these names to the list. ☐

This may make a long list and so you will need to prioritize it until it becomes manageable. Identify ways to reach out and stay in contact with what can become your stakeholder network.

Putting it all together

This final secret pulls all the others together because they all advise working through people and making them your main business. Even people who work alone have customers, suppliers, professional advisers and other people who need regular contact.

Being liked is a challenge when leadership requires you to do and say things that you and other people find difficult. But 'liked' in this instance means more than being popular. It refers to being approachable and trustworthy – someone who deserves respect and who also shows respect to colleagues. Professional liking can occur without knowing anything about a person's private life.

In the same way, dislike is impersonal. People can't really dislike someone they don't know. They can feel annoyed and resentful, but in a superficial way. This makes it easier for leaders to mend situations when they've had to play the tough guy and say no when everyone wanted a yes answer.

Working through and with other people so that they are placed at centre stage makes your job much easier. Not only are you sharing the workload, you're also creating job satisfaction for both yourself and others.

INDEX OF LEADER QUOTATIONS

John Quincy Adams – sixth American president, senator and diplomat
Scott Adams – cartoonist and creator of *Dilbert*
Afrojack (Nick van de Wall) – music producer and disc jockey
Marian Anderson – highly admired contralto-voiced singer of classical music
Maya Angelou – author, poet, dancer and actress
St Thomas Aquinas – saint, philosopher and Catholic theologian
Arapaho – Native American tribe from the Colorado plains
Aristotle – ancient Greek philosopher and scientist
Kristin Armstrong – two-time gold medal Olympic winner for cycling
Mary Kay Ash – entrepreneur and founder of Mary Kay cosmetics
Isaac Asimov – author and biochemist
Marcus Aurelius – second-century Roman emperor and author
Christian Bale – actor and film star
Steve Ballmer – businessman and former CEO of Microsoft
Honoré de Balzac – novelist
Willow Bay – journalist and editor
Sir Cecil Beaton, CBE – Academy Award winner, fashion, portrait and war photographer and painter
Henry Ward Beecher – American anti-slavery campaigner and clergyman
Alexander Graham Bell – scientist, inventor and engineer
Mary Frances Berry – eminent professor of history and author
Niels Bohr – Nobel prizewinner in Physics, quantum theorist
Simón Bolívar – Venezuelan statesman and military leader
Usain Bolt – six-times gold medal Olympic winner for track and field
Erma Bombeck – author and humorist
Napoleon Bonaparte – Emperor of France, military and political leader
Bono (Paul David Hewson) – singer and songwriter for U2
Sir Richard Branson – entrepreneur and founder of Virgin Group
Charlotte Brontë – novelist
Siddhārtha Gautama Buddha – religious sage and founder of Buddhism
Edmund Burke – Irish statesman and philosopher
James MacGregor Burns – historian, political scientist, authority on leadership studies, originator of the leader–follower paradox
Robert Burns – poet and lyricist
Andrew Carnegie – industrialist and philanthropist
Dale Carnegie – writer and pioneer of self-improvement and personal development
Coco Chanel – French fashion designer

Cesar Chavez – American civil rights activist and co-founder of the National Farm Workers Association

Winston Churchill – British prime minister, statesman, historian and author

Hillary Clinton – American senator, Secretary of State and author

William J. Clinton – American president and author

Lord Sebastian Coe – two-time gold medal Olympic winner for track and field

Confucius – teacher, philosopher and politician

William Congreve – playwright and poet

Joseph Conrad – master of English prose and Polish-born British citizen

Alice Cooper (Vincent Damon Furnier) – American singer and songwriter

Stephen Covey – educator, author and businessman

Michael Crichton – author, medical doctor, producer and director

Mos Def (Yasiin Bey) – hip-hop recording artist, actor and activist

Democritus – ancient Greek pre-Socratic philosopher

Felix Dennis – publishing pioneer of computer and hobby magazines and philanthropist

Norma Desmond – character in the film *Sunset Boulevard*

Charles Dickens – author and social critic

Emily Dickinson – poet and pioneer of a simple poetic style

Benjamin Disraeli – British prime minister, statesman and author

Frederick Douglass – social reformer, anti-slavery campaigner and author

Sir Arthur Conan Doyle – author and medical doctor

Peter Drucker – educator and author

Finley Peter Dunne – humorist and author

Amelia Earhart – aviation pioneer and author

Clint Eastwood – actor, director and producer

Thomas Alva Edison – inventor and businessman

Albert Einstein – Nobel prizewinner in Physics and relativity theorist

HRH Queen Elizabeth II – British monarch, Head of the British Commonwealth and Supreme Governor of the Church of England

Ralph Waldo Emerson - essayist, educator and poet

Brian Eno – musician and composer

Werner Erhard – lecturer and author

Harrison Ford – actor and film producer

His Holiness Pope Francis – pontiff of the Catholic Church and Bishop of Rome

Viktor Frankl – psychiatrist, Holocaust survivor and founder of logotherapy

Benjamin Franklin – statesman, author and philosopher

Suzanne Mayo Frindt – author and lecturer

Erich Fromm – psychologist and humanistic philosopher

Robert Frost – Pulitzer prizewinner for poetry, American poet laureate

Indira Gandhi – prime minister of India and stateswoman

Mahatma Gandhi – leader of the India Independence Movement

Bill Gates – co-founder of both Microsoft and the Bill and Melinda Gates Foundation

Charles de Gaulle – leader of Free France, head of the Provisional Government of the French Republic, and founder of the fifth French Republic and its president

J. Paul Getty – industrialist and oilman

Allen Ginsberg – poet and leading figure of the Beat Generation

Arnold H. Glasow – thinker, humorist and generous spirit

Johann Wolfgang von Goethe – poet and dramatist

Vincent van Gogh – artist whose work had a far-reaching influence on twentieth-century painting

Daniel Goleman – psychologist, author and pioneer for emotional intelligence

Steffi Graf – world number one tennis champion and winner of 22 Grand Slam singles titles

Tim Harford – economist, journalist, broadcaster and author of the *Financial Times* column the 'Undercover Economist'

Stephen Hawking – theoretical physicist and cosmologist

Margaret Heffernan – businesswoman and author

Katharine Hepburn – four-time Academy Award winner and American actor

Sir Edmund Hillary – New Zealand mountaineer who with Tenzing Norgay first climbed Mount Everest

Reid Hoffman – entrepreneur, venture capitalist and author

Harri Holkeri – Finnish prime minister and head of the United Nations interim mission to Kosovo

Oliver Wendell Holmes, Jr. – jurist and member of the American Supreme Court

Oliver Wendell Holmes, Sr. – US physician and poet

Reverend Jesse Jackson – American civil rights activist and Baptist minister

Thomas Jefferson – American founding father, principle author of the Declaration of Independence and third president of the United States

Steve Jobs – co-founder and CEO of Apple, author and American entrepreneur

Boris Johnson – British politician and author

Samuel Johnson – poet, essayist, moralist, literary critic, biographer, editor and lexicographer

Tommy Lee Jones – Academy Award winner, actor and director

Ben Jonson – playwright, poet and literary critic of seventeenth-century England

Janis Joplin – singer and songwriter

Carl G. Jung – psychiatrist and inventor of the model of psychological types

Daniel Kahneman – Nobel prizewinner and American psychologist

Rosabeth Moss Kanter – eminent academic, professor and author

Garry Kasparov – chess grandmaster, author and political activist

Helen Keller – author, activist and pioneer for educational rights for the deaf and blind

John F. Kennedy – 35th American president and politician

Sue Monk Kidd – author and inspirational lecturer

Søren Kierkegaard – philosopher, theologian and poet

Billie Jean King – world number one tennis champion and winner of 39 Grand Slam titles

Reverend Dr Martin Luther King, Jr. – inspirational civil rights figure, humanitarian, author and Baptist minister

Stephen King – author of contemporary fiction with 350 million books sold

Eartha Kitt – singer, actor and civil rights activist

John Le Carré (David Cornwell) – author of compelling espionage novels and former British intelligence officer

Ursula K. Le Guin – author, poet and essayist

Abraham Lincoln – 16th American president, leader throughout the American Civil War, and author of the *Emancipation Proclamation* that freed American slaves

Joan Lunden – journalist, author and television host

Douglas MacArthur – American five-star general during the Second World War in the Pacific Theatre

Niccolò Machiavelli – political philosopher, historian, politician and diplomat

Nelson Mandela – South African president, anti-apartheid revolutionary and humanitarian

Jacques Maritain – Catholic philosopher

Abraham Maslow – psychologist and pioneer of the human potential movement; inventor of the hierarchy of needs

Margaret Mead – cultural anthropologist and author

Golda Meir – prime minister of Israel, teacher and author

Eva Mendes – actor and singer

Mary Tyler Moore – actor and comedian

J. P. Morgan – financier, banker and philanthropist

Dorothy Nevill – horticulturist, plant collector and author

Jack Nicklaus – 18-times winner of major golf tournaments

Michelle Obama – attorney, author and American First Lady

Ric Ocasek – musician, music producer and lead vocalist of The Cars

George Orwell (Eric Arthur Blair) – novelist, essayist and journalist

Dolly Parton – singer, songwriter, actor and philanthropist

Blaise Pascal – mathematician, physicist and inventor

Louis Pasteur – chemist, microbiologist, pioneer of vaccination and discoverer of pasteurization

Norman Vincent Peale – proponent of positive thinking

Pelé (Edson Arantes do Nascimento) – football player widely regarded as the greatest player of all time

Plato – ancient Greek philosopher and mathematician

Nicole Polizzi – television personality

Colin Powell – American four-star general, Secretary of State and statesman

Sara Ramirez – singer, songwriter and actor

HRH Queen Rania of Jordan – advocate and Queen Consort of Jordan

Sam Rayburn – American statesman and Speaker of the House of Representatives for 17 years

Ronald Reagan – 40th American president, Governor of California and actor

Jackie Reses – chief development officer of Yahoo

Sir Ralph Richardson – film and stage actor

Eleanor Roosevelt – American politician, diplomat, activist and humanitarian

Theodore Roosevelt – 26th American president, conservationist, historian, author and explorer

J. K. Rowling – author with more than 450 million books sold

John Ruskin – art critic, art patron, watercolourist and philanthropist

Bertrand Russell – philosopher, mathematician, historian and activist

Babe Ruth – 22-season champion baseball player

Carl Sandburg – three-time Pulitzer prizewinner, poet, author and editor

Howard Schultz – chairman and CEO of Starbucks

Dr Seuss (Theodor Seuss Geisel) – author of children's books, selling over 600 million copies

William Shakespeare – playwright, poet and entrepreneur

Anna Deavere Smith – actress, playwright and professor

Steven Spielberg – film director and producer

Bruce Springsteen – singer, songwriter, guitarist and humanitarian

Gertrude Stein – poet, playwright, art collector and pioneer advocate of the modernist movement in painting

John Steinbeck – Pulitzer prizewinning author of *The Grapes of Wrath*, selling 14 million copies

Harriet Beecher Stowe – American leader of the anti-slavery movement and author of *Uncle Tom's Cabin*, an influential book showing the life of slaves

Publilius Syrus – ancient Roman author and playwright

Talleyrand (Charles Maurice de Talleyrand-Périgord) – French bishop, politician and diplomat

Amy Tan – Chinese-American author exploring relationships

Mario Teguh – Indonesian motivational speaker

Mother Teresa (Blessed Teresa of Calcutta, MC) – Nobel prizewinner, missionary and religious sister

Henry David Thoreau – author, poet, philosopher, anti-slavery advocate and conservationist

Linus Torvalds – software engineer and principal force behind the development of the Linux operating system

Harry S. Truman – 33rd American president

Desmond Tutu – South African social rights activist during the anti-apartheid movement, retired Anglican bishop

Mark Twain (Samuel Clemens) – author and humorist

Lao Tzu – ancient Chinese philosopher and poet of ancient China, founder of Taoism, and revered as a deity in religious Taoism and traditional Chinese religion

Sun Tzu – Chinese military general, strategist and philosopher

Jane Velez-Mitchell – journalist, author and television presenter

Leonardo da Vinci – Italian painter, sculptor, architect, musician, mathematician, engineer, inventor, anatomist, geologist, cartographer, botanist and writer

Judith Viorst – author and newspaper journalist

Tom Waits – singer, songwriter, composer and actor

Sam Walton – businessman, entrepreneur and founder of Walmart

John Wanamaker – American politician and marketing pioneer

Booker T. Washington – influential advocate for freed slaves following the American Civil War, author, orator and first leader of the Tuskegee Institute

John Wayne – Academy Award winner, actor, director and producer

Mae West – actor, singer and playwright

Edith Wharton – Pulitzer prizewinning author and designer

Alfred North Whitehead – mathematician, philosopher and defining figure of process philosophy

HRH Prince William, Duke of Cambridge – second in line to the British throne

Tennessee Williams – playwright and author of many stage classics

E. O. Wilson – biologist, researcher, theorist, naturalist and author

Oprah Winfrey – media mogul, actress, producer and philanthropist

William Butler Yeats – Nobel prizewinner in Literature, Irish poet, playwright and politician

Mark Zuckerberg – computer programmer, Internet entrepreneur and one of five co-founders of Facebook

INDEX